The Quest for Moral Leaders

NEW HORIZONS IN LEADERSHIP STUDIES

Series Editor: Joanne B. Ciulla
Professor and Coston Family Chair in Leadership and Ethics,
Jepson School of Leadership Studies, University of Richmond, USA

This important series is designed to make a significant contribution to the development of leadership studies. This field has expanded dramatically in recent years and the series provides an invaluable forum for the publication of high quality works of scholarship and shows the diversity of leadership issues and practices around the world.

The main emphasis of the series is on the development and application of new and original ideas in leadership studies. It pays particular attention to leadership in business, economics and public policy and incorporates the wide range of disciplines which are now part of the field. Global in its approach, it includes some of the best theoretical and empirical work with contributions to fundamental principles, rigorous evaluations of existing concepts and competing theories, historical surveys and future visions.

Titles in the series include:

Moral Leadership in Action
Building and Sustaining Moral Competence in European Organizations
Edited by Heidi von Weltzien Hoivik

Beyond Rules in Society and Business
Verner C. Petersen

The Moral Capital of Leaders
Why Virtue Matters
Alejo José G. Sison

The Leadership Dilemma in Modern Democracy
Kenneth P. Ruscio

The New Russian Business Leaders
*Manfred F.R. Kets de Vries, Stanislav Shekshnia, Konstantin Korotov
and Elizabeth Florent-Treacy*

Lessons on Leadership by Terror
Finding Shaka Zulu in the Attic
Manfred F.R. Kets de Vries

Leadership in Context
The Four Faces of Capitalism
Mark N. Wexler

The Quest for Moral Leaders
Essays on Leadership Ethics
Edited by Joanne B. Ciulla, Terry L. Price and Susan E. Murphy

The Quest for Moral Leaders

Essays on Leadership Ethics

Edited by

Joanne B. Ciulla
University of Richmond, USA

Terry L. Price
University of Richmond, USA

Susan E. Murphy
Claremond McKenna College, USA

NEW HORIZONS IN LEADERSHIP STUDIES

Edward Elgar
Cheltenham, UK • Northampton, MA, USA

© Joanne B. Ciulla, Terry L. Price, Susan E. Murphy 2005

Published by
Edward Elgar Publishing Limited
Glensanda House
Montpellier Parade
Cheltenham
Glos GL50 1UA
UK

Edward Elgar Publishing, Inc.
136 West Street
Suite 202
Northampton
Massachusetts 01060
USA

A catalogue record for this book
is available from the British Library

ISBN 1 84542 534 0 (Cased)

Typeset by Cambrian Typesetters, Camberley, Surrey
Printed and bound in Great Britain by MPG Books Ltd, Bodmin, Cornwall

In memory of our friend and colleague
Fredric M. Jablin
(1952–2004)

Contents

Contributors

Norman E. Bowie is the Elmer L. Andersen Chair in Corporate Responsibility at the University of Minnesota. He is a frequent contributor to scholarly journals in business ethics. His most recent book is *Business Ethics: A Kantian Perspective* and his most recent edited book is *Blackwell Guide to Business Ethics*. His next book *Management Ethics* (Blackwell Publishers) is in press. The seventh edition of his co-edited text *Ethical Theory and Business* was published in 2003. He has held a position as Dixons Professor of Business Ethics and Social Responsibility at the London Business School and been a fellow at Harvard's Program in Ethics and the Professions. He is past president of the Society for Business Ethics, the American Society of Value Inquiry and is past Executive Director of the American Philosophical Association.

Joanne B. Ciulla is Professor and Coston Family Chair in Leadership and Ethics at the Jepson School of Leadership Studies, University of Richmond. Ciulla is a founding member of the leadership school. She has also held the UNESCO Chair in Leadership Studies at the United Nations International Leadership Academy and academic appointments at La Salle, Harvard, and Wharton. Her books include *Ethics*; *The Heart of Leadership*; *The Working Life: The Promise and Betrayal of Modern Work*; and *The Ethics of Leadership*. She recently co-authored a business ethics text with Robert C. Solomon and Clancy Martin called *Honest Work: A Business Ethics Reader*. Ciulla is on the editorial board of *The Business Ethics Quarterly, The Leadership Quarterly*, and *Leadership*. She is editor of the New Horizons in Leadership Series (Edward Elgar).

Jay A. Conger is Kravis Research Professor of Leadership Studies, Claremont College and Professor of Organizational Behavior, London Business School. Conger consults with a worldwide list of private corporations and nonprofit organizations and serves as an advisor and coach to numerous executives and CEOs. Author of over seventy articles and book chapters, and nine books including *Shared Leadership: Reframing the How's and Why's of Leading Others*; *Corporate Boards: New Strategies for Adding Value at the Top*; *Building Leaders: How Successful Companies Develop the Next Generation*; and *Charismatic Leadership in Organizations*.

S.D. Noam Cook is Professor of Philosophy at San Jose State University. His publications, research and consulting interests focus on social and technological change, particularly the roles of specialized knowledge, professional practice and values. He has given invited presentations on his work for academic, industrial and governmental institutions in the US and abroad, including MIT, UCLA, Virginia Tech, Texas A&M, Leiden University in The Netherlands, the University of Westminster in London, MITRE Corporation, Xerox research centers in the US, UK and France, the national government of The Netherlands, and various US federal agencies.

Douglas A. Hicks is Associate Professor of Leadership Studies and Religion in the Jepson School of Leadership Studies and Director of the Bonner Center for Civic Engagement at the University of Richmond. He is author of *Inequality and Christian Ethics* (2000) and *Religion and the Workplace: Pluralism, Spirituality, Leadership* (2003), both published by Cambridge University Press.

Susan E. Murphy is Associate Professor of Psychology at Claremont McKenna College and Associate Director of the Kravis Leadership Institute, currently serving as Interim Director of the Kravis Leadership Institute. Immediately prior to joining Claremont McKenna College, Professor Murphy worked as a research scientist at Battelle, Seattle Research Center. She is co-editor of two recent publications, *Multiple Intelligences and Leadership* and *The Future of Leadership Development* and numerous leadership and mentoring articles. Murphy is co-editor of the forthcoming Lawrence Erlbaum publication *Changing the Metaphor: From Work Family Balance to Work Family Interaction*.

Terry L. Price is Associate Professor of Leadership Studies at the Jepson School of Leadership Studies, University of Richmond where he teaches Ethics, History and Theories of Leadership, and Critical Thinking. He is co-editor of a three-volume set called *The International Library of Leadership*, Edward Elgar Press, and author of *Understanding Ethical Failures in Leadership*.

Robert C. Solomon is Quincy Lee Centennial Professor and a member of the Academy of Distinguished Teachers at the University of Texas at Austin. One of the most prolific philosophers in America, he is the author of over 40 books ranging from Sartre, Hegel, and Nietzsche, to justice, emotions, and a variety of other philosophic subjects. Five of his books are on business ethics, including *Above the Bottom Line*; *Ethics and Excellence*; *It's Good Business*; *A Better Way to Think about Business*; and *Building Trust* (with Fernando

Flores). Solomon is the President of the International Society for Research on Emotion. He has designed and delivered ethics programs for a number of Fortune 500 companies.

Peter Temes is President of Antioch New England Graduate School. He has taught literature, ethics, and writing at Columbia University, Harvard University, the University of Chicago, and other institutions of higher education. His most recent publications include: *The Just War: An American Reflection on the Morality of War*; and *Against School Reform and In Praise of Great Teaching*, as well as articles and book reviews on ethics, education and literature.

Tom R. Tyler is University Professor of Psychology at New York University. He teaches in the psychology department and at NYU Law School. His research explores the dynamics of authority in legal, political, and managerial groups. In particular, he is concerned with the influence of the fairness of the policies and procedures of organizations on the behavior of their members. He is the author of several books, including: *The Social Psychology of Procedural Justice*; *Why People Obey the Law*; *Social Justice in a Diverse Society*; and *Social Influences on Ethical Behavior in Organizations* (editor).

Paul Woodruff is Darrell K. Royal Professor in Ethics and American Society at the University of Texas, Austin. He has written plays, opera libretti, poetry, and short fiction, as well as a number of translations. His novella won an Austin Book Award, and his play won a B. Iden Payne Award for best new play in 1983. His academic publications include a commentary on Plato's *Hippias Major*; *Facing Evil*; and his *Reverence: Renewing a Forgotten Virtue* was published by Oxford University Press in 2001. His translations include Plato's *Symposium* and *Phaedrus,* an abridged version of Thucydides' *History*; *Early Greek Political Thought from Homer to the Sophists*; Euripides' *Bacchae*; Sophocles' *Antigone* in 2001; and Sophocles' *Theban Plays*. His latest book is *First Democracy: Facing the Original Ideas*.

Acknowledgements

This book contributes to a rather small but growing body of literature on the ethics of leadership. Its main goal was to bring new voices, topics, and literature into the discussion of leaders and leadership. We would like to express our gratitude to the Kravis Leadership Institute and Claremont McKenna College for giving the authors in this book a place to present and discuss their ideas at the 2004 Kravis–de Roulet Conference on Ethics and Leadership. The Kravis–de Roulet Leadership Conference is an annual leadership conference funded jointly by an endowment from financier Henry R. Kravis, and the de Roulet family on the campus of Claremont McKenna College in Claremont, California. The 2004 conference was co-sponsored by the Jepson School of Leadership Studies at the University of Richmond and the Peter F. Drucker Masatoshi Ito Graduate School of Management at Claremont Graduate University.

We extend a special thanks to the conference sponsors, Henry R. Kravis and the Vincent de Roulet family, and the faculty and staff who have provided support, as well as the faculty and staff of the Kravis Leadership Institute, who were instrumental in putting together the 2004 conference: Ron Riggio, Susan Murphy, Sandy Counts, Lynda Mulhall, and student interns Yoon-Mi Kim and Kate Oppenheimer. We also owe a debt of gratitude to the Jepson School Research Assistant, Cassie King, for the care and attention to detail that she put into helping prepare this manuscript.

Introduction

Joanne B. Ciulla

The greatest strength and the greatest weakness of leaders is that they are human beings. As such, they are unpredictable creatures, capable of extraordinary kindness and cruelty. They are wise, foolish, careless, reckless, arrogant, and humble – sometimes all at the same time. As the philosopher Immanuel Kant notes, "from such warped wood as is man made, nothing straight can be fashioned."[1] Leaders do not have to live by higher moral standards than the rest of us, but it is imperative that they have a higher compliance rate, because the impact of their behavior impacts on many lives. There are, however, two distinctive factors that make the ethics of leadership different from the ethics of other individuals. The first is power – the way that leaders exercise it and the temptations that come with it. The second is the special moral relationship that they have with followers and the range of people with whom they have moral relationships and obligations.

Leaders have to care about and consider the wellbeing of more people than the rest of us. They have moral obligations to people that they do not know and maybe do not even like. Morality requires this of everyone, but for leaders it is central to the special role that they play. The moral obligations of leaders are painted on a large canvas. Leaders are responsible for the big picture and everything in it. Furthermore, part of any leader's job, in either a small group or as the head of a nation, is to make other people care about something bigger than themselves and help them recognize their own moral obligations. The theme that runs through the chapters in this book is the scope of leaders' relationships to followers and the way that they see themselves in the context of their relationships with the people they lead. Leadership is morality and immorality magnified, which is why we search and hope for moral leaders.

Today, quite a bit of popular and scholarly work centers on extraordinary leaders, on how to be a great leader, and on transformational and charismatic leadership. There are also books on bad and "toxic" leaders.[2] The authors in this collection do not write to praise leaders, nor do they write to disparage them. Our focus is on the complex ethical relationships that are the core of leadership. The quest for moral leadership is both a personal quest that takes place in the hearts and minds of leaders as well as a quest by individuals, groups, organizations, communities, and societies for leaders who are both ethical and effective.[3] The chapters in this book explore the ethical challenges of being a leader and practicing leadership. Some look into the hearts and minds of leaders, and others examine the body of leadership – the way that it is practiced in various groups and organizations.

We begin by looking at the hearts of leaders, which includes their virtues, vices, emotions, and religious beliefs. Paul Woodruff's chapter on leadership in the ancient world reminds us that the quest for moral leaders is an old one that is intimately tied to the values of democracy. People search for moral leaders only when they have some say in the matter. When they have no say, they can only hope for moral leaders or for leaders who will overthrow their bad leaders. Woodruff argues that the ancient Greeks not only developed a concept of democracy, but also a concept of democratic (and, one might argue, moral) leadership. The Greeks defined leadership by clearly characterizing its opposite, the tyrant, who holds total power and rules by fear.

Poets, playwrights, and philosophers of the ancient Greek world had a clear understanding of the human frailties of leaders. At one end of the moral spectrum they identified *hubris* as the main occupational hazard of leaders. Hubris is the pride and arrogance that comes from power and often motivates the strong to take advantage of the weak. At the other end of the spectrum we find reverence, the antidote for hubris. Woodruff tells us that the democratic poets of ancient Greece celebrated reverence because it was the virtue of leaders who recognized the difference between the human and the divine. A reverent leader understands that we all share a common humanity and is conscious of his or her limitations. Reverence, says Woodruff, is the virtue that prevents leaders from abusing their power. Questions concerning hubris and reverence run through all of the chapters in this book.

Power is one characteristic that differentiates leaders from others. It is the key factor that makes ethics particularly difficult for them. The ethical challenges faced by leaders are both intellectual and emotional. In common usage, we only call people *leaders* because they have (willing, or at least not unwilling) followers. Leadership is not a singular concept; it is a complex relationship. As Robert C. Solomon explains, this relationship is not only an ethical relationship but it is also an emotional one – emotions are part of ethics. Niccolò Machiavelli and many authors before and after his time realized that the emotions of fear, pride, resentment, and love, are as much a part of leadership as power, motivation, and vision.

Solomon argues that emotional integrity is the super-virtue of leadership. Emotional integrity is when a person's system of emotions is in balance and he or she has a clear sense of being a part of a larger whole. In some ways, it resembles the Greek virtue of reverence. In his chapter, Solomon talks about the relationship between emotions, ethics, and reason. Often leaders' emotions are far more eloquent and have a greater impact on followers than the rationale that leaders give for their actions and policies. Emotions mask or enhance the way people understand the morality of an action. Solomon notes how difficult it is for leaders to have emotional integrity when the media and professional consultants literally mediate and repackage their emotions.

Solomon's chapter touches on two important themes in leadership literature, charisma and trust. He points out that charisma is not really a quality of a leader, but a set of emotions. These emotions are not necessarily irrational emotions. In the case of good leaders, they are reasonable emotions. We all want leaders whom we can trust and leaders want to be trusted. Solomon notes that this is not simply a matter of finding leaders worthy of trust, but rather a matter of finding leaders who are able to give trust. Often leadership scholars talk about leaders as moral role models. Solomon extends this idea to emotions. Leaders don't just show us how to act; they show us how to feel. Similarly, Solomon says, leaders who project their trust of followers usually have it projected back to them by followers. He says that in the end, the burden of trust is on followers who, like leaders, also need emotional integrity. Followers can be wise or foolish in terms of whom they decide to trust and to follow.

The last chapter in Part One is about religious beliefs. Religion has always been an element of leadership and the way people think about leaders. Most cultures construct their own description of the personality and traits of God or the gods. These descriptions tell us some interesting things about what people in a society think their ultimate leader should be like. Consider, for example, the difference between the way God is described in the Old and New Testaments of the *Bible*. Most religions possess a fervent belief that their gods are the only true gods and many have been willing to kill or die for this idea. Throughout history, some leaders have claimed that they are gods or that they were told what to do by God or the gods. Some have also changed or tried to change followers' religious beliefs or persecuted people for their beliefs. Most religions include the same basic moral principles in their ethical systems, such as prohibitions against killing, lying, stealing, and so on. The way that leaders use their religion to lead sometimes strengthens their moral relationship with followers and sometimes also destroys it. Religion can bring people together or tear them apart.

Douglas A. Hicks examines the question "how should the leader draw upon his or her religious faith as a source of ethical ideas and actions?" Many societies today consist of people from a variety of religions. Since positional leaders have power, their comments concerning faith evoke strong emotions of agreement or concern among followers. The challenge, as Hicks describes it, is for leaders to be able to express their beliefs, but not exclude those who do not share their beliefs. Here again, we see the challenge of moral inclusiveness characterized by both reverence and emotional integrity. Hicks introduces a third kind of inclusion that he calls "respectful pluralism." Respectful pluralism allows for religion in the public life of a leader as long as a leader does not use his or her religious beliefs to degrade or coerce others or to set policies based on religious beliefs that are not shared by everyone. Hicks says that leaders who practice respectful pluralism should not make their religion's position on an issue the official position. A leader's job, according to Hicks, is to create communities where people's religious beliefs can be shared openly and respected.

Respectful pluralism is a tall order for most leaders. One simple strategy for leaders in religiously diverse groups or societies is to make the public space secular and keep their religion private, but Hicks argues that leaders should not have to keep their religious beliefs private as long as they are able to restrict using them to exclude or demean other faiths or to dominate policies. The restrictions of respectful pluralism on faith and the emotions of faith certainly require a tremendous amount of self-control and self-knowledge from a leader who is a true believer. Hicks demonstrates how difficult this is when he discusses how President Bush's public expressions of his faith have fallen short of the requirements of respectful pluralism.

In the first part of the book, we see how religious beliefs and emotions color the way leaders (and the rest of us) make decisions. The second part looks at how leaders think about morality. Terry L. Price raises two questions: should we hold leaders responsible for acting on the wrong moral beliefs and should we hold leaders responsible for moral ignorance? Price points out that many leaders in history such as Stalin, Pol Pot, and Hitler had bad childhoods that may have warped their beliefs about morality and partly explain their behavior as leaders. Other leaders may have grown up in societies where they never learned that slavery, for example, is wrong. Price argues that it would be difficult to let leaders off the hook for bad behavior because they had a troubled childhood, but we may want to cut them some slack if they lived in a society or period of history where they did not learn that certain things were wrong. Price argues that the moral mistakes of leaders fall into two categories. The first is mistakes about the content of morality – that is a leader never learned that slavery was wrong. He says these kinds of mistakes are not difficult to correct. The second kind of mistake is about the scope of morality – who is bound by morality and who is protected by it.

Once again, we see inclusion as a key aspect of moral leadership, but Price shows us another facet to this theme. Some leaders, such as royalty, grow up with special privileges, which may make them feel that they are not included in the group of people who have to follow the rules. As Price notes, even when leaders are not from privileged backgrounds, we grant them special privileges on the job. These privileges may include everything from a fat salary, to perks like private jets and personal assistants, to special access to information and resources. In a provocative twist, Price suggests that when we grant these privileges to leaders, we create situations that make it easy for them to believe that they are outside of the scope of morality by which the rest of society lives. He suggests that by giving leaders privileges or socially constructing leadership as something done from a privileged position, we make those involved in the very exercise of leadership prone to mistakes about the scope of morality. If this is indeed the case, then whom do we hold responsible for the moral mistakes of a leader when that leader does not believe that he or she is subject to the same rules as followers? To what extent are institutions and organizations responsible for the misdeeds of their leaders because of the way that they frame the position and privileges of the leader? And of course, do people sometimes get the leaders they deserve? Notice that this is more than a question about due diligence and checks and balances. It extends into the fuzzy territory of how we create images of and contexts for leaders that make it especially difficult for them to behave morally.

The next chapter in this section offers a concrete illustration of some of Price's concerns about the privileges that we afford leaders. Jay A. Conger writes about how executive power and compensation can corrupt business leaders. Like Price, Conger does not think that all immoral business leaders are simply bad apples in a barrel. The larger problem, says Conger, is that the barrel is broken. In his chapter, he shows how structural problems in American corporations (such as cases where a CEO is also the chairman) fail to provide the right checks and balances. However, he also points to two psychological phenomena that contribute to the problem of what Price calls "special privileges." The first, according to Conger, is called "the romance of leadership," which is when people over-attribute control to leaders because they prefer to feel that someone rational is in control rather than to believe that events are controlled by fate. Business books and the media feed into this by turning successful business leaders into heroes and celebrities. The second psychological phenomenon is the growing number of narcissistic corporate executives. These narcissists are highly competitive, they constantly benchmark themselves with others, and they believe the romancing the leader myth. Top executives rationalize their high salaries by using the equity theory of compensation, namely that they deserve to be paid as much as others in their position. This not only creates a sense of privilege for one leader, but for a whole class of CEOs, who in turn sit on each other's boards and approve each other's salaries.

Conger highlights some social trends that have made corporate executives more susceptible to moral mistakes that stem from what Price calls scope problems. Corporate leaders used to take a social entity view of the corporation, which meant that the corporation had a moral obligation to distribute wealth throughout society. They were much less likely to see themselves as exceptions or deserving huge salaries and perks when they thought of their obligations in this context. Nowadays, executives hold a property conception of the corporation, which means that their primary obligation is to make profits for stockholders. Under these conditions, Conger says, it is much easier for executives to ask for huge compensations because profits are private, not social goods. As things stand today, it is not considered unethical for a CEO to make a lot of money, especially if it is tied to performance, but as we have seen in business scandals, it is often the celebrity CEO with the excessive paycheck who commits some of the most unethical deeds. Corporate executive compensation has gotten so enormous, in comparison to other workers' salaries, that it has made it difficult for the public to believe that the CEO has the company's interests at heart. This is one reason why the public has lost faith in the integrity of business leaders.

Peter Temes' chapter takes us on a somewhat different tack. Sometimes leaders have to do bad things. Perhaps this is one of the most emotionally and intellectually difficult parts of being a leader – knowing when to do something that is ethically wrong but in the interests of those served. Ethics is about acting on moral principles, but it is also about knowing when it is right to violate a moral principle. For example, killing is wrong, but there are circumstances, such as self-defense, where killing is necessary. Moral principles are precarious. We violate moral norms with great care lest we lose the habit of following them. Some of the most difficult decisions leaders make involve what Peter Temes calls the problems of dirty hands and necessary sin. Leaders have dirty hands when they make a deal with a ruthless person, but deliver something good to their constituents – to some extent the ends justify the means. Temes says that in these cases, the leader's conscience is clean because he or she has at least delivered the goods. The necessary sin leaders are not as fortunate. They choose between two evils, but also sacrifice their own sense of being a person who does good instead of bad acts.

Both dirty hands and necessary evil sound like nothing more than the ends justifying the means, but they are not. These kinds of decisions leave behind a remainder of wrong. They do not let you off the moral hook. Killing people to save lives is still killing people. Killing people is still morally wrong, even if that is what one has to do. Nonetheless, because leaders sometimes have to make these kinds of decisions, Temes offers guidelines for committing necessary sins. The first involves identifying the good in terms of the distinction between acts that improve people's wellbeing, but not necessarily their happiness. Leaders often have to make decisions that their followers do not like. The second entails isolating what really matters, which requires looking at the problem in a broader context, whereas the third, and perhaps most controversial, guideline involves thinking about morality at the level of the person rather than the group. In this way, Temes incorporates both utilitarian principles and a corrective to utilitarian excesses. By thinking about morality as it applies to each individual, a leader is better able to consider the variety and scope of his or her constituents.

Part Three of the book shifts our attention to leadership in organizations. The quest for moral leaders is also a quest for leaders who motivate (or simply allow) followers to be ethical too. Like ethical leaders, ethical followers should, in their own capacity, care about others in a community, group, or organization. In Tom R. Tyler's chapter, we see how a leader's ethics influence the work of people in an organization. Tyler's chapter is quite different from the rest of the book, but it complements the others by empirically testing the relationship between ethical leadership and effective leadership in organizations in the "real" world.

Motivation is a key element of leadership. Tyrants motivate by fear, and in modern organizations leaders motivate people with money and status (and sometimes fear). One reason why vision is so important to leadership is because a compelling vision contains more than a common end or goal. It consists of a rationale for why an end or goal is good in some larger context. Morality is a powerful motivator and an extremely powerful de-motivator. When people complain about their jobs, it is usually because they feel that they are either not being treated with respect or because they are not being treated fairly. Solomon argues that followers reflect the emotions of a leader. Tyler's study illustrates how followers reflect their perception of the leader's ethics. If a leader does not treat people with respect and fairness at work, workers may not treat their jobs and the organization with fairness and respect. Creating justice, fairness, and trust in the workplace (and elsewhere) is a full-time job, especially because leaders have to make dirty hands decisions, such as firing people when business is bad. From the workers' or followers' perspective, the ethics of leaders and justice in the organization are major components of motivation and commitment. Tyler's study tells us what we all hope is true – namely that ethical leadership works better than tyrannical leadership.

As we see from Tyler's research, the ethical relationship between leaders and followers takes place in a large system of variables and relationships. S.D. Noam Cook's chapter offers a systems perspective of leadership ethics. From a systems point of view, a leader's job is to provide and maintain the infrastructures that make public discussion of ethics possible. Cook agrees with Conger that unethical behavior is not simply a matter of bad apples. If you only focus on the individual, you overlook the question, what in the system made that bad apple possible? Cook argues that it is the leader's job to maintain an infrastructure that allows for discussions of ethics and safeguards the participation of all people affected by that discussion. By its very nature, a human system cannot flourish unless any potential interventions in it consider all of its parts and how those parts are related. Furthermore, human systems cannot flourish without taking into account how they interface with other systems.

According to Cook, all human systems have values infrastructures, where moral discourse takes place. Leaders should oversee the infrastructure, but they should not dominate it. Cook says leaders need to know when to interfere with a conversation about ethics and when not to interfere. Like sailors, they have to be careful that they do not "oversteer" the system. When a leader over-steers the ethics conversation, he or she may stifle healthy discussion. Cook believes that the best leadership occurs when the constitution is sound, the team is well trained, and the orchestra is well rehearsed. When a human system is well prepared both ethically and technically, then leaders can move from the stance of intervention to stewardship. In other words, well-constructed and maintained systems of good followers yield the best leaders. Cook thinks Henry David Thoreau got it right when he said, "government is best which governs not at all."

A systems approach to leadership measures the health of the organization by the extent to which it flourishes. Norman E. Bowie uses a related concept to evaluate good leadership – sustainability. The leadership and business literature is filled with articles about change, but perhaps this is because leaders are either unwilling to maintain, or incapable of maintaining, healthy organizations. Bowie agrees with Conger that the excessive focus on share-holder value has been detrimental to the ethics of business leaders. While Conger discusses this in terms of compensation, Bowie talks about the responsibility of business leaders to take into account other stakeholders. Again, we see questions about how a leader sees his or her scope of moral obligations.

Bowie ties the scope question to the personal virtues of a leader. The virtues of a sustainable business leader are related to reverence. They are empathy, humility, and personal resolve. Using James Collins' image of the window and the mirror, Bowie says that great leaders look out the window when things go well, to see who is responsible, and they look in the mirror when things go wrong. Bowie observes that one rarely sees a humble person involved in a business scandal.

Bowie also argues that you cannot separate the character of a private person from the public leader. Great business leaders, observes Bowie, also seem to be moral in their personal lives. He offers a series of examples of unethical business leaders, from Bernie Ebbers to Martha Stewart, who had morally problematic personal lives. They offer some nice illustrations of people who do not think that they have to play by the rules. They also raise questions about emotional integrity and ethics. Do these leaders have a kind of emotional integrity – rotten at home and rotten at work? Is it possible for bad people to do good things as leaders? Bowie struggles with these questions, especially when it comes to the case of President Clinton's affair with Monica Lewinski.

There is something almost unnatural about being an ethical leader. Several aspects of leadership defy normal inclinations. We naturally care about and are willing to make sacrifices for friends, family, and neighbors, but leaders frequently have obligations to strangers and communities outside of their own. Their job often requires them to serve the interests of a variety of strangers and groups over their own interests and the interests of their families and friends. Morality requires this of all of us sometimes, but once again, this requirement is inherent in what it means to be a leader and to do the work of a leader. Ethical leadership is, for most leaders, a constant quest to keep a perspective on who they are, how they relate to the group, and to whom they have obligations. It entails a level of self-knowledge and self-control that is challenging to sustain over time and under the pressures of the job. Ethical leaders have to be above the crowd and yet one of the crowd.

Leadership ethics encompasses much more than the content of a leader's values. Ethical values and norms are always in motion at the center of how leaders do their jobs. Justice, fairness, duties, and the greatest collective good are more than just values and beliefs. They are the currency of all leader/follower relationships. While this book is not designed to praise leaders, it should help the reader understand why we treasure the good ones. Moral leadership is both difficult to find and difficult to sustain.

NOTES

1. Immanuel Kant, "The Idea for a Universal History with a Cosmopolitan Intent," in T. Humphry (ed. and tr.), *Perpetual Peace and Other Essays*, Indianapolis, IN: Hackett Publishing Company, 1983, p. 34.
2. See: Barbara Kellerman, *Bad Leadership: What it is, How it Happens and Why it Matters*, Boston, MA: Harvard Business School Press, 2004, and Jean Lipman-Blumen, *The Allure of Toxic Leaders*, New York: Oxford University Press, 2005.
3. Joanne B. Ciulla, "Ethics and Leadership Effectiveness," in John Antonakis, Anna T. Cianciolo and Robert J. Sternberg (eds), *The Nature of Leadership*, Thousand Oaks, CA: Sage Publications, 2004, pp. 302–27.

PART ONE

The hearts of leaders:
virtues, feelings, and faith

1. The shape of freedom: democratic leadership in the ancient world

Paul Woodruff

Ancient Greece, in the fifth and fourth centuries BC, was developing a concept of leadership along with the concept of democracy. Of the many democracies that emerged in this period, only one is recorded in any detail, and we are lucky enough to know this one very well. The city-state of Athens was far from perfect democracy, but it was founded on ideals that deserve our attention today. This chapter is based on a larger study of the goals of ancient democracy.[1]

After the battle on the plain of Marathon, the Athenian commander dedicated his helmet to Zeus at Olympia. It is still there. You may see it in the museum, its classic shape almost intact, its inscription still legible: "Miltiades dedicated this." The Athenians won at Marathon in the year we call 490BC, less than twenty years after the dawn of an experiment in democracy, which was to be increasingly successful over most of the next two centuries, before it was put down by the larger armies of Macedon after the death of Alexander the Great. It was never a perfect democracy. The freedoms that the men of Athens cherished they never extended completely to women or foreigners, and they denied it to slaves altogether. Still, democracy helped Athens become the most successful Greek city-state of its time. And along with the idea of democracy came the idea of a kind of leadership that is compatible with freedom.

Miltiades and the army of Athens had been astonished by their victory over the Persians. The Persian army, they believed, was ten times more numerous, and it had always been victorious. Behind it, all of the Greeks it visited had capitulated or been conquered by its superior force. The city of Athens was so unsure of winning the battle that it might well have surrendered as soon as the Persian fleet rowed into sight. That is why Pheidippides had to run all that way – the distance we now call a marathon – to tell the people of Athens that they had won the battle on land, that they must not give up now.

Of course they thought the gods had helped them, and heroes too had risen from the dead to help save their beloved city. That explains the dedication at Olympia. Gods helping mortals is an old idea, but a new thought soon pushed its way to the forefront of people's minds. Athens had been a democracy for eighteen years at the time of the battle. Its army was an army of free men, led by a general the people had elected. They were opposed by an army that they saw as an assembly of armed slaves who were whipped into battle by a tyrant.

What was it that gave each Athenian the strength to defeat ten Persians? Freedom, the Athenians thought, their new freedom – this was what had made them so powerful. And so victory at Marathon encouraged them to believe that they had taken the right road. They discovered the enormous value of freedom on the plain of Marathon.

"Freedom" by itself is a hungry word; it hasn't the strength to mean anything unless it is fed. First, "freedom" has to absorb a clear idea of the alternative – of what it means "freedom *from*." As the ancient Greeks came to appreciate the value of freedom, they also came to see that tyranny – which in former times had been a neutral word for one-man rule – was an evil. The freedom of Athens was freedom *from* tyranny.

Second, "freedom" is not a full-blown concept unless it is beefed up by a clear sense of what it means "freedom *for*." Simply not having a tyrant is not very much; mere "freedom-from" is shapeless. It is as vague as "escape." Where is it headed? What will it do? Who will give it direction? What, in a word, is it freedom *for*? The answer that fed meaning into the word "freedom" for the Athenians was that of full participatory democracy. Rich and poor alike were acquiring access in Athens at this time to all the tools of power – so long as they were male citizens. This restriction had serious consequences, of course, but I will not discuss them here. Citizens comprised most of the manpower in the Athenian forces, although resident aliens did military service, and slaves sometimes fought along side their masters. (Indeed, the entire police force of Athens consisted of slaves.)

From this notion of freedom, now well-fed, it follows that when the Athenians went into battle, they followed not a tyrant, but a leader, and they followed him as free men who had been involved in his choice and would hold him accountable for his failures. Like freedom, leadership has negative and positive sides.

THE NEGATIVE SIDE: LEADERSHIP IS NOT TYRANNY

The negative side is what a leader is not. A leader is not a tyrant. Evil often seems more clearly defined than good, so writers not surprisingly found it entertaining to say what a tyrant is, and therefore to show what a leader is not. The word "tyrant" did not carry a negative image until the age of democracy. Before that, it simply meant a monarch, sometimes a monarch who had not inherited his job. The ancient word that came to mean "legitimate king" (*basileus*) had been used for various kinds of leaders, most notably for judges.

The earliest description we have of tyrannical behavior is from the *Iliad*, which shows Agamemnon abusing his power over Achilles. Much later, in the democratic period of Athens, the tragic poets picked up the theme and sounded it in a more political context. These stage tyrants are endangered; neither their people nor their gods entirely support them.

The ancient tragic poets of Athens, who are the main voices for democracy that have survived from this period, are eloquent about tyrants. By "tyrant" they mean a monarch who places himself above the law and tries to maintain power by frightening his citizens; he is afraid that someone will displace him violently, and so he requires a bodyguard (unlike legitimate kings and democratic leaders in this period). The chief mark of the stage *tyrannos* is fear: he rules, and is ruled by, fear. A related mark of the stage tyrant is his *hubris* – the arrogance that comes from unlimited power and an absence of reverence.

Hubris has become accepted as an English word that means arrogance or overweening pride. But this does not fully capture what the word meant to the ancient Greeks. Any outrage committed by the strong against the weak is called *hubris*; *hubris* is not only an attitude, it is a kind of action as well. Rape or sexual harassment would count as *hubris*. More generally, *hubris* is a violation of anything or anyone held to be sacred or to be under the special protection of the gods. The opposite of *hubris* is reverence, which is the primary virtue of leaders in the ancient scheme of values. At the same time, reverence is the quality that tyrants most conspicuously do not have. In all cases, violations of reverence are more conspicuous than are acts of reverence, with the result that reverence has been an elusive concept.

Reverence (as celebrated by the democratic poets of ancient Greece) is the felt recognition of the difference between the human and the divine. Reverent leaders know that they do not have divine powers or divine knowledge, and they act accordingly. Irreverent potentates forget their humanity. Under the illusion that they know what is right all by themselves, they ignore advice that might save them. They do not listen to their people. Under the illusion that they can control everything around them, they turn to violence when violence is ineffective. One stage tyrant – Pentheus in Euripides' *Bacchae* – tries to suppress an ecstatic religion by putting its leader in prison. Another – Creon in Sophocles' *Oedipus at Colonus* – tries to force Oedipus to bless his own side in a civil war by kidnapping Oedipus' daughters. But no blessing can be forced, and no prison has ever contained a religious movement. *Hubris* gave these tyrants the illusion of powers they did not have; reverence would have taught them to be mindful of their limitations. This lesson the democratic Athenians learned and relearned by watching tragic plays at religious festivals.

Performances of tragic plays in Athens supplied a large part of the education of Athenian citizens in political matters. Virtually all citizens participated in dramatic festivals, which were an essential element in the civic and religious life of Athens. As young men, citizens were recruited to dance in the choruses; rich men paid for the productions as a public duty; and (for part of Athens' history) poor men had their entrance fees paid out of a public fund (the *theoric* fund). We do not know whether women attended the performances, but there is some evidence that they did.

Athenian audiences liked to see democratic values supported in the theater, and they were fortunate in the poets who appealed to their taste. Aeschylus, Sophocles, and Euripides all addressed issues in democracy in thought-provoking ways. The plays are never pedantic. Instead of pushing a clearly defined political line, they raise hard questions. The stage tyrants are clearly paving the way to their own catastrophes in most Greek tragedies; nevertheless, they are often attractive figures. Oedipus is especially engaging; in him Sophocles illustrates how close *hubris* can be to qualities we rightly admire. Creon too, in the *Antigone*, is a good man trying to do the right thing. A tyrant is not a villain. He is tragic: tragic because the mind in him that set its aim on good leadership goes slightly off course, often because he is trying so hard to do the right thing. The choices that ethical leadership calls for are not simple, not black and white, and the great tragedies illustrate them in all the complexity of their competing colors.

I have already mentioned two examples of stage tyrants – Pentheus in Euripides' *Bacchae* and Creon in *Oedipus at Colonus*. Creon is a better man in Sophocles' more famous play, the *Antigone,* but he is still a tyrant. In such plays, tyranny typically leads to blindness, which leads to *hubris*, which leads to catastrophe. Pentheus loses sight of the limitations of his power and commits an outrage by attempting to imprison someone he thought is a leader of a new cult. In fact, it is the god Dionysus whom Pentheus tries to restrain. Dionysus works within Pentheus' mind to unhinge him still further, and he later inspires Pentheus' mother literally to tear her son apart.[2]

Creon is a two-dimensional tyrant in *Oedipus at Colonus*, which shows him violently trampling on the laws of god and man. Like Pentheus, he lacks reverence, and shows this in his cruel treatment of the weakest people in his power – suppliants. (A suppliant is a refugee with no hope aside from the reverence of his or her host.) In the *Antigone*, Creon is more complicated. He accepts the idea of the rotation of leadership positions and he occasionally listens to his council of elders.[3] Still, he treats the dead without reverence, denying burial to a dead boy, and, like all tyrants, he shows himself unwilling to listen to people who disagree with him.

THE POSITIVE SIDE: LEADERSHIP SUITS DEMOCRACY

The positive side is what a leader is. On this subject the ancient texts are less helpful. I think I know why the ancient writers found leadership hard to explain: democratic leadership requires democratic followers. Leaders of a given kind will not surface in a society without the appropriate kind of followers. You cannot describe a form of leadership without describing the entire form of community that allows for it. On this larger question, the ancient sources have a fair amount to say. But the tragic plays use stories set long before the age of democracy, and this leads to paradox. The character who is the foremost apologist for democracy in the plays that have come down to us is Theseus, and he is also the clearest example of a leader, as opposed to a tyrant. But Theseus was a king in the mythology of Athens, albeit a legitimate one. Nevertheless, he was a hero of a democracy that detested monarchy in all its forms, and no one seems to have been upset by the paradox. Theseus is a model leader in Sophocles' *Oedipus at Colonus*, where his main role is to exemplify the values of Athens while serving as a foil to Creon. In Euripides' *Suppliant Women*, Theseus gives the most eloquent defense of democracy that has come down to us (lines 403–8 and 426–56).[4]

From such passages we may draw the following sketch of the kind of leadership that is compatible with democratic freedoms. Leaders represent justice and reverence in their public and their private lives. These virtues help leaders to serve under law, to accept the rotation of leadership positions, and to be content with close public scrutiny of their actions. Such ideal leaders are not afraid of being replaced, do not think they are uniquely qualified for their positions, and have nothing to hide. They respect the opinions of others, along with the qualifications of other citizens to lead.

In order to understand what this means, we need to keep in mind the main features of ancient democracy, as it was understood in theory:

> Positions of power are given by lot, and are held subject to public examination.
> All issues are brought to the public [for deliberation].
> (Herodotus, *History*, 3.80, GW, pp. 83–4)

The passage comes from a debate about forms of government, which is cast in terms familiar to ancient Athenians. When Herodotus wrote it, he imagined it taking place in ancient Persia, but its ideas are entirely Greek.

First, the lottery. In Athens, some offices were held by election, but Athenians knew that elections were distorted by wealth and family background, as rich aristocrats tended to have an edge over ordinary citizens. Ordinary citizens, however, were frequently elevated by the lottery to temporary positions of power, and this system worked well in Athens for nearly 200 years. The lottery guaranteed that ordinary citizens would participate, and it could act as a damper on any voting majority. Second, the public examination. Public officials were accountable to the people both through the judicial system and through special boards of examiners. In addition, any citizen could prosecute an office holder, if he could afford to put up a deposit, which would be forfeit if the case were judged frivolous. Third, public decision-making. Athens had an Assembly, which had final word on issues of law and policy. Any citizen could vote, speak or make a proposal in the Assembly. But the Assembly's power was limited by three representative bodies selected by lot. The Council had to pass on any business before it came to a vote in Assembly; this was a pre-deliberative body (like US Congressional Committees), of 500 citizens chosen by lot equally from the ten tribes. Legislation could be framed only by a second body, also selected by lot, known as "Lawmakers" (*Nomothetai*). In addition, anyone who made an unconstitutional proposal was subject to a charge that brought on judicial review by a large jury – often 501 citizens selected by lot. Any citizen could bring a charge of unconstitutionality against any speaker in the Assembly.

Obviously, you would have to develop a moral character of a certain kind, if you were to lead effectively in a system with rotating offices, strict accountability, and public decision-making. We shall see that justice and reverence – two moral virtues with ancient pedigrees in Greek thinking – emerged as the most important virtues underlying the ancient concept of democratic leadership.

The most famous leader of democratic Athens was Pericles, but I will not take him as a model leader in this chapter. One historian wrote of him:

> The reason for Pericles' success was this: he was powerful because of his prestige and intelligence, and also because he was known to be highly incorruptible. He therefore controlled the people without inhibition, and was not so much led by them as he led them. He would not humor the people in his speeches so as to get power by improper means, but because of their esteem for him he could risk their anger by opposing them. . . . Athens was in name a democracy, but in fact it was a government by its first man. But because those who came after were more equal among themselves, with everyone aiming to be the chief, they gave up taking care of the commonwealth in order to please the people. (Thucydides, *History* 2.65, GW, pp. 101–2)

The author of this encomium does not like democracy very much; he admires Pericles precisely because he thinks that Pericles is not really a democratic leader, but a sort of monarch in disguise. The encomium cannot be quite true; Pericles was brought to trial and convicted on a charge not known to us (probably some kind of corruption), and his imperialist policies were crowd pleasers from the start. He was a savvy elected politician who rewarded the voters with an expanding (and not very democratic) empire, a rich public works program (including the Parthenon), and a system of payment for service on juries. He clung to office for many years, winning election after election. Admirable in many ways, disturbing in others, he is not an ideal example of democratic leadership as understood at the time. He serves better as an example of how easily elected leadership – as opposed to rotating leadership – can diverge from the democratic ideal.

In the following sections, I examine in more detail the ancient concepts of tyranny and leadership.

WHAT A LEADER IS NOT: SYMPTOMS OF TYRANNY

The idea of tyranny is among the greatest gifts we have from ancient Greece, because it nails down a vital way to think about freedom. The ancient Greeks realized that tyranny is a kind of government that destroys a people by dividing them, while it weakens leaders by clouding their minds. The leader may be a person or a group, and tyranny may rise in what is nominally a democracy. Tyranny is the enemy of freedom:

> Whoever traffics with a tyrant
> Becomes his slave, even if he came as a free man.
> (Sophocles, Fragment 873, GW, p. 58)

Tyranny may be a popular form of government even so. Some early Greek tyrants rose to power by taking the side of the poor in civil conflict. And, as a matter of history, tyrants were not always bad. The Athenian tyrant Pisistratus, for example, is said to have ruled wisely under the law. Had he ruled otherwise, however, the Athenian people could have done little to protect themselves, for Pisistratus had an armed guard.[5]

On the theatrical stage of democratic Athens, tyrants are usually bad news, though not without exception. Oedipus is clearly labeled a tyrant in Sophocles' *Oedipus Tyrannus*, and shows many signs of tyrannical behavior. But he is also a thoughtful, caring leader of his people, and his passion for self-knowledge is admirable. Still, the tyrannical features of his rule are destructive both to himself and to harmony in the city. His fear of losing power leads him to angry suspicion against two men who are important to the city and are trying to help him – his brother-in-law (and uncle) Creon, and the city's infallible, but often incredible, prophet Tiresias.[6]

Like a disease, tyranny is recognized by its symptoms. These symptoms are the features of political leadership that the ancient Greeks most feared. And the Greeks were right to fear them. If you observe any of these symptoms in your leaders, be wary. The political equivalent of a plague could be on the way, and it could weaken your freedoms fatally. For each symptom, I cite a text or two illustrating how it is presented on the democratic stage of Athens.

A tyrant is afraid of losing his position, and his decisions are affected by this fear. That is why tyrants may find themselves treating their own friends as enemies, and that is the main reason, according to ordinary Athenian wisdom, that they were thought to be miserable.

> . . . You won't find anything more miserable.
> You'll have to ruin and kill all your friends,
> For you will live in greatest fear if you do not.
> (Sophocles, Fragment 608, GW, p. 71)

> . . . Do you think anyone
> Would choose to rule in constant fear
> When he could sleep without trembling,
> And have exactly the same power? Not me.
> Why should I want to be Tyrant?
> I'd be insane . . .
> (Sophocles, *Oedipus Tyrannus*, Creon speaking, lines 584–9)

> . . . When the people govern a country,
> They rejoice in the young citizens who are rising to power,
> Whereas a man who is king thinks them his enemy
> And kills the best of them and any he finds
> To be intelligent, because he fears for his power.
> How then could a city continue to be strong
> When someone plucks off the young men
> As if he were harvesting grain in a spring meadow?
> (Euripides, *Suppliant Maidens*, lines 442–9)

A tyrant tries to rise above the rule of law. Although he may give lip service to the law, a stage tyrant's ambition and rapacity are not contained by law, and such a tyrant thinks himself as free as a god to do what he will. The rapacity of tyrants became proverbial, and this, on top of their fears, made them liable to overstep the law.

> All the gold of Gyges means nothing to me;
> I've not yet been seized by envy, I do not admire
> What the gods do, and I do not want to be
> A great tyrant. These things are beyond my sight.
> (Archilochus, Fragment 19, GW, p. 22)[7]

> Nothing means more evil to a city than a tyrant.
> First of all, there will be no public laws,
> But one man will have control by owning the law,
> Himself for himself, and this will not be fair.
>
> *   *   *
>
> Why should one acquire wealth and livelihood
> For his children, if the struggle is only to enrich the tyrant further?
> Why keep his young daughters virtuously at home,
> To be the sweet delights of tyrants . . .?
> I'd rather die than have my daughters wed by violence.
> (Euripides, *Suppliant Maidens*, lines 429–32 and 450–55, GW 65)[8]

The conception of law that underlies this symptom of tyranny is crucial. Ancient Greeks in general would reject the idea that the law is whatever the authorities say it is. In other words, they did not accept a purely positive account of law. Their notion of law was closely woven into their traditional morality.

A tyrant does not accept criticism. A striking example comes from Sophocles' *Antigone*. Creon's son Haemon tries tactfully to persuade Creon to call off the execution of Antigone, but Creon lashes out at him, unable to see Haemon's argument as anything but an attack on him and his leadership:

> *Creon*: It turns out this boy is fighting for a woman's cause.
> *Haemon*: Only if you are a woman. All I care about is you.
> *Creon*: This is intolerable! You are accusing your own father.
> *Haemon*: Because I see you are going wrong. Because justice matters.
> *Creon*: Is that wrong, showing respect for my job as a leader?
> *Haemon*: You have no respect at all if you trample on the rights of gods!
> (Sophocles, *Antigone*, lines 740–45)[9]

A further symptom of Creon's failure is his confusion about respect and reverence. He demands respect for himself, as leader, but he seems blind to the need to show reverence to the gods, or to treat the dead with reverence. I shall return to this theme.

A tyrant cannot be called to account for his actions. You have no more power to punish a tyrant than you have of punishing bad weather – that is, unless you set out to assassinate him or remove him by force of arms. In Athens, two men were goaded to fury by the harassment of a tyrant, the younger son of Pisistratus. They got past his bodyguard and killed him, but both died for this (one at the moment and the other after torture). The older son continued as tyrant, but his days were numbered, and the two tyrant-killers became heroes; their statues had a place of honor in Athens.[10]

A tyrant does not listen to advice from those who do not curry favor with him, even though they may be his friends. We have seen that Oedipus was unable to take advice from Tiresias or Creon. He was equally reluctant to take advice from his wife. This is partly because of his obsession with knowledge, but must be attributed also to his lack of trust in other people:

> For this plague always comes with tyranny:
> That the tyrant does not trust his friends. (Aeschylus, *Prometheus Bound*, lines 224–5, Prometheus speaking)[11]

WHAT A LEADER IS: THE SHAPE OF FREEDOM

A democratic leader is supposed to be everything that a tyrant is not. Such a leader is content with public decision-making. A leader of this sort is not afraid of being replaced, is not too rapacious to submit to the law, is willing to take criticism, accepts accountability to the people, and is able to take advice from people who disagree.

Participation for All

> The people [*dêmos*] are lord here, taking turns
> In annual succession, not giving too much
> To the rich. Even a poor man has a fair share (*ison*).
>   This is freedom: To ask, "Who has a good proposal
> He wishes to introduce for public discussion?"
> And one who responds gains fame, while one who wishes
> Not to is silent.
> What could be fairer than that in a city? (Euripides, *Suppliant Women*, lines 406–8, 437–41)

In the early years of democracy, many aristocrats sought to subvert public decision-making. They felt that their position in society – or their wealth – gave them a right to a kind of leadership that democracy did not permit. Twice the aristocrats staged coups in hopes of ending democracy, and twice they were defeated. After the second defeat, both parties swore an oath of reconciliation and amnesty. The Assembly accepted certain limitations on their power, and the aristocrats were content for nearly a century to lead, as opportunity permitted, under democratic rules.

Leadership Under the Law

The law that constrains leaders has three features. First, it is allied to traditional morality and not changed arbitrarily by any powers that be. Second, it is written, so that leaders cannot deceive the people about what it requires. Third, it applies to all citizens equally; leadership never gives you privileges before the law.

> When the laws are written down, then he who is weak
> And he who is rich have equal justice:
> The weaker ones may speak as ill of the fortunate
> As they hear of themselves, and a lesser man
> Can overcome a great one, if he has justice on his side. (Euripides, *Suppliant Women*, lines 433–7)

The very people who seem to make laws justly do not really abide by the laws they make and enforce:

> A wolf who had been made general over the other wolves established laws for all, so that whatever any of them caught while hunting he would bring to the whole

pack and give an equal share to everyone, so that the rest would not eat each other out of hunger. But an ass came forward, shaking his mane, and said, "That was a fine plan from the mind of a wolf. But how is it that you put yesterday's kill back in your den? Bring it to the whole pack, and divide it into shares." Thus exposed, the wolf repealed the law.[12]

Too bad; it was a good law, and a good leader would have had the character needed to retain it even though it was to his personal disadvantage.

Reverence

We have seen that the vice of tyrants is *hubris* and that the opposing virtue in leaders is reverence, as this was understood in ancient Greece. Reverence is mainly a felt sense of human limitations. Reverent leaders will not let their power fool them into thinking that they are wise enough to go forward without advice. Reverent leaders also recognize the limitations they share with the weakest people who are in their power. Reverence, in this understanding, is what holds back the strong hand of power from abusing the weak. There is nothing else, after all, to hold you back, if you have the highest power in the neighborhood, except your own goodness. And the goodness the Greeks prayed for in their leaders was reverence.

> Wisdom? It's not wise
> To lift our thoughts too high;
> We are human, and our time is short.

So sings the chorus in Euripides' *Bacchae* at the center of a hymn to reverence (lines 395–7). They have chosen this theme because the king of the city in which they find themselves has gone too far. He has attempted to suppress a religious movement by force of arms, a movement that has just now erupted in his city. He is too sure of himself to take advice, too sure of himself to admit that setting military force against religion might backfire. Reverence would have saved him; if he had had enough of it, he would have felt the need of advice, felt the inadequacy of his power at this moment. The Athenian audience, watching the play, would have known all this; they would have seen the play – among other things – as a reminder of the high price leaders pay for forgetting to be reverent.[13]

Others also pay a high price for a leader's irreverence. Often (but not in democracy) leaders have so much power that they have nothing external to save them from abusing their power. Their only hope – and our only hope if we are under them – is that they are held back by some internal constraint. Internal constraints on behavior are called virtues, and they were at the center of ancient Greek ethical thinking. The classical theory of virtue is worked out by Aristotle in his *Nicomachean Ethics*, but he did not invent it out of whole cloth; he was articulating the wisdom about virtue that had developed up to his time, towards the end of the age of democracy. A virtue modulates your emotions at the source, so that if you have a virtue, you feel like doing the right thing, and you would feel ashamed of doing the wrong thing. If you have courage, for example, you will take pleasure in courageous actions; you will want to take them, and you will be averse to cowardice.

This classical understanding of virtues clashes with some modern ideas about courage, which would count you as courageous only if you did the courageous thing while *not* feeling at all like doing so. If you prefer the modern idea about courage, ask yourself this: would you feel safer going into danger with a friend who would really feel like doing the brave thing, if called upon, or with another friend who would have to overcome a great aversion to risk before coming to your assistance? Ancient ethicists set the highest value on the person whose goodness is most reliable, not on the person who has to work hardest in order to be good.

The virtue that prevents the abuse of power is reverence. So we learn from the poets of this period and other literary writers. Plato and Aristotle were not interested in this virtue, but, much later, Stoic philosophers took it up as an admirable quality. Reverence prevents the abuse of power by helping powerful people remember their own vulnerabilities and their own limitations; it helps them see what they have in common with helpless people to whom they might do harm. Without reverence, we might find it easy to imagine great differences between us and our potential victims, and to use those differences to insulate us from any revulsion against the abuse of another human being. When otherwise good people abuse prisoners, this is partly a failure of imagination – a failure to see them as fully human. But the deeper cause is a failure of reverence – a failure to see ourselves as the fallible, vulnerable human beings that we are.

Reverence need not occur in a religious context; its effect is primarily on the way human beings treat each other. In a religious context, however, it governs people's respect for the line between the sacred and the profane. In ancient Greek culture, helpless people were held to be sacred in an important sense, because they had nothing but their special status to protect them. Suppliants (people we would call refugees), prisoners, aging parents, the dead – all these fall behind a line which even a powerful monarch is not supposed to take violence.

Democracy, as we have seen, has structural ways of keeping leaders in line. But even in democracy these are not sufficient. Think of all the circumstances in which we might have others in our power, so totally that we would have no fear of being called to account. In modern times, consider the power of a policeman stopping an underprivileged teenager on a dark night in a lonely place. Or attendants in a nursing home, alone with a patient who is not far from death. Or, not so very long ago, think of the power of a priest over an altar boy. It still matters to us, as it did to the ancient Greeks, that people who are given power are taught to be reverent.

Justice

Justice looms large in the moral discourse of the ancient Greek world. Except for a few outliers like the character Thrasymachus in Plato's *Republic*, no one seems to doubt that justice is a good thing, and everyone seems clear about what it requires – keeping promises, paying debts, taking no more than one's fair share, punishing the guilty. There was some debate about how practical it was to be just, especially in war and in maintaining an empire, but I will not discuss that here.[14] Democratic leaders are bound to follow the way of justice because of their commitment to the rule of law, and the Greeks of this time generally thought that law was supposed to express justice.

What is specific to leadership, however, is the way that it brings justice about – not through force, not merely through law, but by something far more powerful:

> It is clearly better to promote moral virtue by means of exhortation and persuasion than by law and compulsion. For someone who is deterred from injustice by law will probably do wrong in secret, but someone who is led to do his duty by persuasion will probably not do anything improper either secretly or openly. Thus the person who acts correctly out of understanding and knowledge becomes both courageous and straight-thinking.
> (Democritus, Fragment 181, GW, p. 160)

And Hesiod, almost as ancient a poet as Homer, describes the power granted to "kings"[15] (in their capacity as judges) as coming from a divine source, just as his audience believed that poets and bards could win over an audience because of the gift of song that they had from the muses.

Calliope keeps company with kings who are held in awe,	80
And if the daughters of great Zeus should honor and watch	
At the birth of one of the kings who are nourished by Zeus,	
Then they pour sweet honey on his tongue, and the words	
From his mouth flow out in a soothing stream, and all	
The people look to him as he works out what is right	85
By giving resolutions that are fair: he speaks out faultlessly	
And he soon puts an end to a quarrel however large, using his skill.	
That's why there are kings with intelligence: so they	
Can turn things around in the *agora* [marketplace] for people who've suffered	
Harm, easily, persuading them with gentle words.	90
As he comes to the hearing, like a god they seek his favor	
With respect that is soothing, and he stands out from those assembled.	

Such is the holy gift the Muses grant to human beings.
It's from Muses, you see, and from Apollo far-shooter
That we have men on earth who sing or play the lyre.   95
True, kings are from Zeus, but anyone prospers if he's loved
By Muses: then his voice flows sweetly from his mouth.
And when someone grieves and is newly troubled in spirit,
While pain withers his heart, then, even so, if a singer
Who serves the Muses will sing out the glory of bygone men   100
And the joys of the gods who dwell on Olympus,
Then he will soon forget his troubles and not remember
His cares, as the goddesses' gifts quickly grant him a change.
(Hesiod, *Theogony*, 80–103, GW, pp. 19–20)

This would be the noblest and the best that leadership can achieve – to
bring a peaceful end to a quarrel, to use words so beautifully that the anger and
grief behind a quarrel are spirited away. All too often such powerful leadership
seems impossible to find, and yet every now and then it emerges, summoning
people to higher causes than remembering old quarrels. The ancient Greeks
knew that that the highest goal of leadership is the unity of those who are led.[16]

NOTES

1. Paul Woodruff, *First Democracy: The Challenge of an Ancient Idea*, New York: Oxford
   University Press, January 2005. Because this chapter is largely an epitome of work I have
   published, I cite mainly my own works here. Readers will find in them guides to further
   reading and research, along with more thorough citations.
2. For an account of the various interpretations of the play, and a general bibliography, see my
   Euripides Bacchae (Indianapolis: Hackett Publishing Company, 1998).
3. See the introductions to these plays in Peter Meineck and Paul Woodruff, *Theban Plays*
   (Indianapolis: Hackett Publishing Company, 2003).
4. For a convenient translation of these lines with other texts bearing on democracy, see
   Michael Gagarin and Paul Woodruff, *Early Greek Political Thought From Homer to the
   Sophists* (Cambridge: Cambridge University Press, 1995), hereafter abbreviated GW,
   pp. 62–5. In this play, Theseus speaks also for ideas implicitly related to democracy – the
   value of reverence (214–18, GW, p. 63) and the importance of the middle class (238–45,
   GW, p. 63).
5. See Solon's fragments 9 and 11 (GW, pp. 28–9), and Thucydides 6.54. On civil war as a
   prelude to tyranny, see Theognis 39–52 (GW, pp. 31–2).
6. For a thorough discussion of the meaning of the word "tyrant" in this period, see Lowell
   Edmunds, "Oedipus as Tyrant in Sophocles' *Oedipus Tyrannus*," *Syllecta Classica* 17,
   (2002), pp. 63–103.
7. Archilochus was a Greek poet of the eighth and seventh centuries BC. Unless otherwise indicated, the authors quoted in this chapter are Athenian writers from the period of democracy.
8. Compare the fragment from Euripides' *Antigone*: "To rule without law, to be a tyrant, is
   neither reasonable (*eikos*) nor right" (GW 70).
9. For a complete translation of *Antigone*, see Meineck and Woodruff (2003).
10. Thucydides is the source of this story, in his *History of the Peloponnesian War*, 6.54–59. For
    an abridged Thucydides, see Paul Woodruff, *Thucydides on Justice, Power, and Human
    Nature* (Indianapolis: Hackett Publishing Company, 1993).
11. Translated by the author for *First Democracy* (Woodruff 2005).

12. "General Wolf and the Ass." This translation of Aesop is from GW, p. 146.
13. For a more detailed account of reverence in leadership, see my *Reverence, Renewing a Forgotten Virtue* (New York: Oxford University Press, 2001).
14. This is a large theme in Thucydides. See especially his Melian dialogue (5.84–114; GW, pp. 118–25), where the Athenians claim that justice is irrelevant to the war at hand (but notice that they do not claim that might makes right). See also Pericles' famous remark that their empire is like a tyranny: though it seemed unjust to take the empire, it would be unsafe to give it up (2.63; GW, p. 100).
15. "Kings": the traditional English rendering of *basileis*, which could in this context be translated "lords" or "judges." In Hesiod these are not monarchs, and they do not seem to have any functions other than judicial.
16. This is not reserved only for democratic thinkers. It is a major theme in Plato's work, from the *Republic* through the *Statesman* to the *Laws*. And yet no form of government depends more on the harmony of the people than democracy, as the Athenians discovered at the end of their civil war in 403 BC. See my *First Democracy*, Chapter 4.

2. Emotional leadership, emotional integrity[1]

Robert C. Solomon

the leader is in the realm of transcendence, Beyond the inessential freedoms. He decides. And a mysterious grace makes his decision what is essential. (Jean Paul Sartre, *Notebooks for an Ethics*, p. 10)

Leadership is about people's emotions. People are moved by their emotions. People are motivated by their emotions. People are "swayed" by their emotions. People make decisions on the basis of their emotions. (Indeed, recent research has shown quite convincingly that rational decisions are quite impossible without emotions.[2]) What's more, emotions are "contagious." They affect other people, not just by virtue of the consequences of emotional behavior – that is very obvious – but our emotions determine, often by way of a demonstrably sub-rational and unconscious route, others' emotions as well. An inspirational leader spreads his or her enthusiasm, virtually *injects* it, into his or her followers. And more generally, an atmosphere of enthusiasm generates more enthusiasm, as laughter generates more laughter, as anger and indignation generate more anger and indignation, as despair generates more despair. Whatever else an effective leader does, whether he or she makes people think, or remember, or act, he or she makes others *feel*, whether pride or hatred or indignation or love or fear.

Accordingly, there has been considerable interest in the role that emotions play in leadership, but most of it has been interest in the emotions of followers, the emotions inspired, evoked, or provoked by leaders. Thus Aristotle, in his *Rhetoric*, literally wrote the book (or the first of many books) on how to move your audience to fear and anger. Niccolò Machiavelli pondered whether a prince is better served by inspiring love or fear in his subjects.[3] And the German sociologist Max Weber spent considerable energy discussing *charisma*, which may have been a mysterious trait of great leaders but whose effects were clear and evident in his or her followers. I, personally, have discussed at some length *trust*, which, again, is cashed out mainly in terms of the trust of followers (leaving aside the difficult question of the supposed trustworthiness on the part of the leader). And, more generally, politicians as well as political theorists want to know, for obvious reasons, what excites people, what moves them, and in what directions. In 2004, many Americans said that they voted for George W. Bush because they "liked him" or "felt comfortable with him," not passionate emotions, perhaps, but emotions all the same – but what about the emotions of the leader?

It is the emotions of the leader that, in addition to his or her actions and decisions, inspire the emotions of his or her followers. Often, in a popular leader, these emotions are identical. A leader's compassion inspires compassion in his or her followers; a leader's anger inspires anger in his or her followers; a leader's shame inspires shame in his or her followers. Of course, sometimes, the emotions inspired may be in opposition to the leader, who may also inspire suspicion, fear, indignation, anger, and even hatred. And sometimes discomfort on the part of the followers may motivate them to distance themselves from their leader, or turn against him or her, for instance, if the leader confesses shame but his or her followers are unwilling to share that shame. I want to suggest that it is a mistake to put all of the focus on the followers, for it is the emotions of the leader that are in question. The most effective form of leadership is for a leader to inspire through his or her own emotions, providing not just an example but an inspiration for his or her followers. The most effective contribution to emotional leadership is for the leader to display emotional integrity.

Emotional and ethical leadership might be construed in such a way as to generate a paradox. (Philosophers love to begin with paradoxes, as a way of clarifying what is at stake.) The paradox is this: leadership is all about emotions, both the emotions of the leader and the emotions inspired by the leader, but ethics, it is often argued, has everything to do with rationality (rational principles, categorical imperatives, the principle of utility, or based on fair and rational procedures), but rationality and emotion have long been opposed to each other. In fact, emotions (and the broader traditional class of "passions") have often been considered not only "irrational," but antithetical to rationality. If that were the case, then emotions have nothing to do with – or are by their nature opposed to – ethics. So, leadership is by its very nature unethical (or not ethical) and ethical leadership is something of a contradiction in terms, like "jumbo shrimp."

I would want to resolve this paradox, obviously, in the direction of genuine ethical leadership that is also emotional. The concept of emotional integrity is intended to do just that. First of all, I would want to insist that leadership is not *all* about emotions, and second, that ethics is not *all* about rationality. What is most important is that emotions are not as such irrational but, quite to the contrary, embody reason. As Nietzsche writes, "As if every passion doesn't contain its quantum of reason." It is not just a "quantum." I have argued at length elsewhere[4] that emotions are essentially structured by judgments and therefore embody all sorts of "reasons," which is why we can say that someone's anger is unreasonable, his jealousy is unjustified, her love is foolish, and that there is no reason to feel ashamed or guilty. Emotions often involve keen insight, whereas reason and reasoning that is unanchored in emotion often wanders off the point or finds itself just plain uninterested (as opposed to "disinterested," which has to do with not playing favorites). Antonio R. Damasio and others have shown that damage to the part of the brain that controls emotion renders a person utterly incompetent at making the simplest decision, even though their reasoning and memory are intact.[5] In other words, there is no rationality without emotion, interest, and caring. Thus, I would want to say that ethical leadership is both about emotions and rationality – it's about having the *right* emotions that are appropriate to the circumstances and the people who are being led. And ethics is, at least in part, about principles that are grounded in the right kinds of emotions, that is, love and compassion, but also a keen sense of justice and, where appropriate, moral indignation.

I would also want to deny the exclusivity of those descriptions of ethics, and consequently of ethical leadership, that put all of their emphasis on principles and procedures. Granted, principles and procedures have their place, but they are not the whole of ethics and they do not explain why ethical leadership is so often considered quite independent of such matters, most obviously when we praise a leader for being "pragmatic" or "sensitive to the needs of his or her followers." The missing piece of the picture is what is usually referred to as "character." I have long defended what is widely known as "virtue ethics" in the realm of business ethics and, now, in leadership studies. Virtue ethics focuses on the notion of character as central to ethics and leadership. Like the notion of integrity, to which it is closely tied, character should not be understood as an isolated feature of the person but rather in context as a feature of his or her relationships and sociopolitical roles. Furthermore, character should not be distinguished from actual performance. It is all too easy for a leader to pose as a person with integrity. Action and responsibility establish whether one has integrity. "Actions speak louder than words," we often hear, and this is particularly important in leadership. Whether one has emotional integrity is much more than integrating one's emotions. It is how one expresses those emotions in the world, not just in words but in behavior. Thus, my defense of ethical leadership will be couched in the language of virtue ethics. And the concept that I want to focus on is what I am calling emotional integrity.

WHAT IS EMOTIONAL INTEGRITY?

Emotional integrity, I want to argue, is the key to the virtues and, based on the Confucian theory that good leadership is virtuous leadership, integrity is essential to good leadership. What is integrity? In *A Better Way to Think about*

Business,[6] I argue that integrity is a kind of super-virtue, a synthesis of virtues rather than a virtue as such. Emotional integrity, accordingly, is not an emotion but a system of emotions in balance, a way of handling one's emotions but, more important, a way of cultivating one's emotions in a kind of effective harmony. The word "integrity" means "wholeness," wholeness of virtue, wholeness as a person, wholeness in the sense of being an integral part of something larger than the person – the community, the corporation, society, humanity, cosmos. Emotional integrity is also wholeness as a person and wholeness in the sense of being an integral part of something larger than oneself, a wholeness in which leadership plays a natural role. Indeed, from the point of view of emotional integrity, the very distinction between leader and follower involves a deep misunderstanding. The leader already encompasses his or her followers. He/she is part of them and they are part of him/her. Integrity thus suggests a *holistic* view of ourselves, although the word "holism" has suffered considerably from New Age excess and has accumulated a consequent aura of fuzziness. Consider the emotion of love, which I have argued must be understood not so much as "I *and* thou" but *(à la* Martin Buber) a holistic "I–thou" relationship. Thus, we should resolutely decide Machiavelli's either/or in favor of love rather than fear, for fear marks an obviously antagonistic rather than holistic relationship.

Integrity is often thought to refer to a person's "inner" coherence and consistency. This makes the notion of "emotional integrity" more plausible, as emotions, too, are typically thought of as "inner." I think that this is problematic, both in regard to integrity and emotions. Integrity may have something to do with what is supposedly "inside" a person, that is, their thoughts, feelings, beliefs, desires, ambitions, and moods, but I would rather say (for reasons that will become evident) that these are features of the person rather than mysterious states "inside" the person. That is to say, I reject the "Cartesianism" that is often implicit in these discussions and with it the divide between "inner" mind and "outer" behavior. Integrity is the integration of the features of the person and their behavior, the fact that these make sense in terms of one another, and the integration of their personal features and their behavior. In good Wittgensteinian fashion, I want to say that emotional integrity is a public phenomenon, even when it is private. That is, our emotions are not "in" either the mind or the head, and though they no doubt have their causal substratum in the brain, it is not as if they are just neurological processes either. Our emotions are "out there" in the world, in our relationships and interactions with other people. An emotion is not something distinct and separate from its expression, but, as many recent psychologists have argued (and not necessarily with a behaviorist bias), the expression *is* the emotion. There is also a feeling, of course, some more or less distinctive experience that is specific to that emotion. As Wittgenstein suggested, the feeling plays no significant role in the emotion. We are not Cartesian homunculi actors on an "inner" stage, making ourselves known to the outside world only when we choose to. We are citizens of the world, and we navigate our social environment wearing our emotions like a psychological skin, sometimes hidden behind a suit of expressive masks but perfectly evident to anyone who pays close attention.

Integrity is also understood as resisting or refusing the orders of others, the idea being that integrity shows itself only when it is challenged. In a tradition that goes back to Kierkegaard and Nietzsche, but is very much at home in America from Henry David Thoreau to Martin Luther King, integrity means resistance, and in particular resistance to the unenlightened "herd" (in Kierkegaard and Nietzsche's nasty formulation[7]). Just as often, however, integrity requires obedience and loyalty. As "wholeness," integrity has just as much to do with one's coherent connections and relationships with other people and institutions as it does one's relationship to oneself. These are, of course, *emotional* relationships, at least in part. So, emotional integrity consists in part in the coherent and, to some degree, intimate connection and identification with other people. This is particularly important in leadership. The leader's emotional bonds with his or her followers are utterly essential. They are not simply a "plus" to his or her leadership capabilities. This means, of course, that they have the right emotions, the proper degree of intimacy, and the optimal scope to their relationships. An administration that prizes loyalty within the inner circle but makes it a mere matter of tribute for those outside the circle violates the demand for optimal scope. The optimal scope for a leader's relationships should include all those who are led. Here we must also consider, what are the right emotions in these relationships? Going against what I suggested in earlier parts of the chapter, I would warn that love is not always appropriate as the central relationship emotion. Respect and compassion are often more appropriate, and love at a distance too easily becomes mere idolatry.

When one willingly joins a group or an organization, he or she agrees to act on its behalf and in its interests and agrees with its aims and values. Obedience and loyalty are part and parcel of integrity. The key, of course, is that the group or organization and one's role and one's position should be compatible with one's own values and virtues, and vice versa. When one comes to disagree with those aims and values, integrity may require disobedience and disloyalty, and perhaps resignation. This is no less true of the leader than it is of anyone else. Leaders do not usually create groups or organizations from scratch, and even when they do, the group or organization soon evolves a personality, a structure, and values of its own, which may or may not be those of the leader. This makes it seem as if "integrity" has two very different meanings, one of them encouraging conformity and obedience, the other urging a belligerent independence,[8] but this is misleading. Integrity includes both one's sense of membership and loyalty and one's sense of moral autonomy. "Wholeness" means that one's identity is not that of an isolated atom but rather the product of a larger social molecule, and that wholeness includes – rather than excludes – other people and one's social roles. One might say (not too misleadingly) that talking about emotional integrity makes explicit the fact that leadership is necessarily about the quality of relationships.

Unfortunately, the word "integrity," like "honor" (its close kin) has suffered considerable abuse in recent years, particularly in politics. Politicians with no integrity claim it for themselves, indeed, insist that they have integrity just because they say that they do. Even worse, those who display integrity are often blasted (sued or even indicted) for it, called "traitors" or "cowards" and accused of disloyalty. In the current climate of cynicism "integrity" has come to seem all but archaic, overly idealistic, "unrealistic." Such is also the case for emotional integrity, which is wrongly accused of emotional rigidity, emotional intractability, or emotional isolationism. True, integrity is what endures through change and trauma. It is, in that sense, something that can only be measured by virtue of some test. Every leader seems fine when things are going well, when he or she is riding high in the polls, when opposition is minimal, and the parades are marching. It is the times when the economy tanks (and "spin" won't hide it), when the poll numbers sag, when the opposition is screaming, and the parades (those not sponsored by the party in power) have stopped, that test leaders. Conflict is the test of emotional integrity. (Compare Nietzsche's famous aphorism: "That which does not kill me makes me stronger."[9]) Emotional integrity is a not just a flood of like-minded emotions, capable of overpowering any opposition, but the ability to navigate a flood of treacherous emotions through the cultivation of emotional harmony.

EMOTIONAL INTEGRITY AS UNITY, COHERENCE AND CONSISTENCY

Insofar as emotional integrity is *integrity*, the emotional integrity of a leader would seem to be established by a singularity of vision and intent, for example, not resting until Britain wins the war or not allowing fear and greed to sink an already frail economy. Singularity of vision and intent may not be enough for emotional integrity. What frequently passes as "ideology" is in fact emotionally single-minded obstinacy or, worse, a self-willed emotional blindness to the needs and concerns of other people. Singularity of vision and intent may also involve denial and dishonesty, neglect of one's family or one's personal life more generally, and neglect of the public good because of an obsession with that single goal. Or much worse, what if that single-minded goal is to single-mindedly stay in power? Consider a Saddam Hussein or a

Robert Mugabe who ruthlessly pursues this goal, and for several decades succeeds, at great cost and causing enormous suffering among his own people. I hope that no one would call this emotional integrity. Here, let me make the point I only hinted at earlier in the chapter: integrity as wholeness need not be simple consistency (a "hobgoblin of little minds," wrote Emerson), nor does it require coherence. Integrity and emotional integrity are matters of *complexity*. Coherence applies to complexity, of course, but it does not entail or imply anything like a simple fit or a simple-minded system. A leader who knows only one or two responses to any crisis or threat is not thereby demonstrating emotional integrity but emotional simple-mindedness. This may or may not be admirable (depending on the nature of those responses) but it is not emotional integrity. The results of such emotional simple-mindedness may even be excellent (for example Ronald Reagan's single-minded attacks on the "evil empire," which shortly thereafter collapsed). That alone is not sufficient for emotional integrity. (Thus it is important that Reagan's exemplary personal life was typically the subject of discussions of his character, not his one-dimensional Cold War foreign policy.) Emotional integrity is most evident in extremely delicate and complicated crises, where simple solutions are foolish or inappropriate, where it is perfectly proper (even obligatory) to have "mixed feelings," and it is in handling such mixed feelings that emotional integrity is exemplified. By contrast, emotional single-mindedness may well be a symptom of emotionally immature and dysfunctional leadership.

Emotional integrity in leadership involves what in virtue ethics is typically called "self-mastery," which includes keeping one's emotions in check, cultivating the *right* emotions, and the ancient ideal of inner harmony. In their discussions of virtuous leadership, both Confucius and Plato, among many others, emphasize the importance of emotional integrity in this sense. "Harmony" is an apt metaphor for the emotional complexity that makes for emotional integrity. Harmony can be extremely complex, including counterpoint which is more than just harmony but involves the inter-weaving of sometimes conflicting lines of melody. So, too, emotional integrity in leadership often involves the ability to deal with conflicting lines of obligation and necessity and both personal and political as well as large-scale prudential emotional demands. Thus emotional integrity is not just the "inner" part of us. It is more than personal tranquility, it is essential to virtue, which means one's character and one's dealings with others and, in the case of leaders, with the world at large. Thus, emotional integrity is doubly important to good leadership, both because it prepares the leader for the emergency and conflict-ridden situations that are bound to arise and because it is a mechanism for dealing with such situations. One might say that leadership magnifies emotional integrity, as it mercilessly displays the lack of it.

It is unfortunate that Americans often focus on the personal virtues and character of their leader rather than his or her virtues on the job – not that the two will be all that divergent. (That, in itself, would suggest a serious lack of coherence and emotional integrity.) It is easy enough for most people to understand troubled family relations, or personal friendships, or the temptations of adultery, and very difficult to understand the kinds of institutional and political pressures and the complications of diplomacy and protracted negotiations involved in leadership. The same virtues that make a person an excellent leader might also cause difficulties in his or her personal life. Certainly one's personal virtues (for example in one's family) do not translate into excellent leadership and may well make leadership impossible.

Emotional integrity does display a certain unity (as the term would suggest) but it is by no means a simple or simplistic unity. It requires flexibility as opposed to rigidity and presupposes a kind of self-confidence that goes far beyond the confidence that a leader might have in the weapons at his command or the support of his immediate supporters and advisors. Some of this self-confidence, of course, depends on the confidence of those who are led. The causal interaction is two-way or, perhaps we might say, that confident leaders and confident followers are the *yin* and *yang* of effective leadership. Moreover, the virtues and the emotions of an effective leader are typically "contagious." An effective leader provides a role model for his or her followers. Confident leaders often have confident followers. Nonetheless, it is necessary to have the *right* emotions, and the right kind of self-confidence. Resentment and envy are typically poisonous in a leader and even more so when they are picked up by the followers. Luckily, most Republicans, much less most Americans, did not share Nixon's resentments. His resentment and envy, resulting in a kind of paranoia, eventually turned off all but the most ideologically committed of his supporters. Slobodan Milosevic's resentments, by contrast, gripped his nation and made them genocidal.

The self-confidence discussed above is thus itself a largely emotional phenomenon, involving both the right emotions and the emotional strength and flexibility to deal with conflicts of emotion. Coherence of policy depends on this. But coherence in policy does not mean simple coherence of emotions, and here is where self-mastery becomes all-important. Self-mastery, and consequently emotional integrity, might be seen as a kind of psychological juggling act, but one in which one has such personal confidence (meaning not confidence in the outcome but the confidence that one can handle the probable contingencies) that while the outcome may be entirely uncertain, the leader's ability to handle the situation is not. Hence, emotional integrity in leadership involves "knowing oneself" (though this is by no means so straightforward as it may sometimes seem). I insisted that the emotional integrity of both leaders and followers depends on having and inspiring the *right* emotions, but now we should add that the right emotions may be dependent on one's own sense of self and the particularities of the situation. Those who confuse rigidity with integrity ("he stands by his principles") tend to ignore the flexibility that is essential for leadership. This is not to defend a vulgar pragmatism, much less to condone emotional opportunism, but to insist that emotional integrity is both situation-oriented and character-based.

As uncomfortable as Americans tend to be with pubic displays of emotion, they tend to expect a spirited response to issues and to unfair criticism. It is a delicate matter of what psychologists call "display rules." As presidential candidate John Kerry countered attacks on his military service record by fighting back – in anger. And yet, the news story said, "For voters who are just getting to know Kerry, the risk is that he comes across as a man who is angry, or tense, or given to harsh language." Joanne Ciulla suggested that "Kerry needs to learn to strike back without seeming angry: We don't want presidents to get mad. We want them to be stern but not mad"[10] – a delicate balance indeed.

THE "CHARACTER" QUESTION

Virtue ethics in leadership studies, I said, focuses on the notion of *character* as central to ethics and leadership, but much of what I have said here throws the familiar notion of character up for grabs. Character is not an isolated feature of the person but more of a summary virtue, a measure of how well all of the virtues operate together. (Thus Aristotle and later the Stoics defended a notion of "the unity of the virtues," which might be interpreted as an early conception of emotional integrity.) Emotional integrity, accordingly, does not depend on any particular emotional disposition but rather on the way that all of the emotions operate together (although the emotions, to be sure, must also be appropriate and "right" for the situation). Once again, character and emotional integrity cannot be separated from action. Almost all leaders try to pose as persons of integrity, even the most vicious and evil of them. The test of emotional integrity is in the doing. People may be seduced and swayed by glorious words and imaginative and merely imaginary plans, but sooner or later – one hopes sooner – they come to insist that words be made into deeds, and that imaginative plans be implemented. Virtue is another concept that should not be interpreted as a Cartesian "inner" as opposed to a political "outer," namely action. Leaders may speak the language of morality and integrity, but what we demand is morality and integrity, which is not just a matter of posture and presentation. Character and emotional integrity cannot be divorced from their expression in action.

The ideal of emotional integrity also hits what might appear to be an insurmountable obstacle in current discussions of leadership. I have been talking as if the character of the leader is something more or less straightforward, one might say, "unmediated." But our knowledge of our leaders is rarely direct and unmediated. It is mediated – to be trite – by the media, by image-makers, and by political "handlers." (A frightening and degrading concept, if you think about it.) A few decades ago, this was a novelty and fairly primitive. Today, it has become pervasive. Rarely does a leader or would-be leader speak on his or her own, express his or her own opinions, show his or her own emotions. Public behavior and expression is poll-driven, media-determined, and thoroughly strategic. We rarely see our leaders "in action." We see "photo ops" that, at best, symbolize actions. We rarely see honest expressions of emotion, except, perhaps, that rare and usually embarrassing display of anger (although more often than not, that is choreographed as well). Nor do we get much of a chance to meet our leaders in person. We see images of our leaders, or personal "appearances," which is not the same thing at all. Five minutes of conversation with a leader is often a stunning (and sometimes utterly depressing) experience. (Richard Pryor after briefly meeting with Ronald Reagan during his second term in office said, "Man, we in trouble.")

Forty years ago, Marshall McLuhan wrote, "Politics will eventually be replaced by imagery. The politician will be only too happy to abdicate in favor of his image because the image will be much more powerful than he could ever be" (quoted in *The Nation*, 12/29 p. 25). This condemns our appraisals of both character and emotional integrity to tedious detective work, requires critical acumen and some courage on the part of the media. For most people, estimates of a leader's character and emotional integrity become matters of faith, in some cases all too literally. (It is shocking to see that the "divine right of kings" has resurfaced in contemporary democracy, as leaders claim for themselves divine privilege – and are so designated by their faithful followers.) It is hard to know what to make of the virtual reality of much of leadership, and it is a very real concern whether the media that demands our trust is in any way worthy of it.

Character is now created, not in the existential fashion that insists, *à la* Jean-Paul Sartre, that "man makes himself" but in the more confusing and degrading sense that it is the image of character rather than character that counts. Bill Clinton's political enemies exposed (after a great deal of expense and trouble) his extra-marital proclivities (if that's the word). George W. Bush's supporters advertised his "integrity" by way of nothing more than capitalizing on his marital fidelity and his late-found religiosity. In retrospect the American public came to realize that there is more to a leader's integrity than avoiding sexual peccadilloes (or being caught in them).

One knows a leader by his or her effects on followers. Indeed, leadership and followership are *yin* and *yang*, mutually defining. For example, Renana Brooks (in *The Nation*, 6/30/03 and 12/29/03) argues that Bush is cultivating "a nation of victims" and cultivating a sense of loss of control and perpetual crisis. And ironically, this sense of helplessness feeds a seemingly contradictory need for personal defense and self-mastery, manifested in the pathological gun craze that is usually attributed to our macho society. Here we must remember Machiavelli's question and his subsequent advice: should the Prince choose to rule through love or fear? He says fear, but it need not be the fear of the Prince. There is, perhaps, no more effective leadership ploy than generating a pervasive fear that cannot be pinned down or even identified (except by reference to other ghost forms, Osama bin Laden and Saddam Hussein). And when it is unidentifiable pervasive fear that is presented along with an identifiable savior, all questions of character and emotional integrity go out the window.

CULTIVATING EMOTIONAL INTEGRITY

Emotional integrity is not a static emotional state, nor is it something that some lucky people have when they are born. Emotional integrity, like the emotions themselves, is largely cultivated. Some of this is just developing emotional self-restraint and self-control, which is one of the features of emotional intelligence.[11] But much of it has to do with integrating several related features of our emotional lives, which nevertheless must first of all be distinguished. They are: emotional integrity vs. emotional sincerity vs. emotional consistency vs. emotional authenticity vs. emotional spontaneity. These are all what we might call "meta-emotional character traits" but they play different roles and serve different functions in our psychological economy. Emotional integrity, as I said, requires flexibility and resilience. Emotional sincerity, by contrast, has to do with emotional transparency, veridical self-knowledge, and genuineness. Thus a person is emotionally sincere if he or she is "in touch with" his or her feelings, if he or she is honest about them, and if his or her expressions are straightforward and revealing of his or her emotional state. In a leader, accordingly, emotional sincerity may be problematic. It is essential that a leader has this quality in his or her personal understanding and responses, but it is doubtful that such an honest transparency would be at all suitable in a serious leadership position.

Emotional consistency, as I suggested above, has the great virtue of predictability, but, again, this may be a mixed blessing in positions of leadership. Personally, it may be essential (so long as consistency isn't confused with rigidity). But given the demands of strategy, it may sometimes be self-defeating in public negotiations. (Nixon's "madman" strategy is an extreme example.) Emotional consistency, we might say, involves flexibility in response to changing circumstances but a consistent and therefore predictable emotional stance to ward the world. But emotional integrity is more than this. It also involves flexibility in one's emotional stance.

Emotional authenticity, like emotional integrity, invokes values. It has to do with having the right emotions, but in this case, emotions that are in tune with one's objective values. In other words, emotional authenticity is strictly normative and has to do with one's ability to give personal authorization to his or her emotional responses (in addition to taking responsibility for them and honestly expressing them).

Emotional spontaneity, finally, has to do with the ability to show non-deliberative, more or less automatic emotional responses. This does not conflict with the idea that our emotional responses are or should be cultivated rather than simply "natural," but there is also "second nature" such that our cultivated emotional responses may nonethess come to be "natural" in the sense that there is no inhibition or hesitation in our emotional expression. Emotional spontaneity is an essential aspect of a leader's ability to inspire trust, in particular, and it may also be a primary ingredient in that hard-to-get-hold-of phenomenon called "charisma." A leader may have emotional integrity but display it only deliberatively and at cost of some pain. Emotional spontaneity thus supplements emotional integrity in a most important way.

CHARISMA RECONSIDERED

In one of my earlier essays,[12] I expressed serious doubts about the value of celebrating charisma as a way of understanding leadership, first of all (as I argued above) because it seems to focus more on the effects on the followers than on the virtues of the leader him or herself, second, because it has religious origins which by their very nature are difficult if not impossible to tie down. Thus "charisma" was, unfortunately, without obvious ethical value (vicious leaders may be loaded with charisma) and without much explanatory value either. It is one of the most frequently occurring terms in current discussions of leadership. The term comes (in its current usage) from Max Weber. It is one of the only terms that explicitly captures the emotional quality of leadership. I believe that the term emotional integrity provides a more constructive and encompassing way of appreciating the emotional quality of leadership. In Weber, in particular, the very notion of charisma connotes an irrational as opposed to a rational influence (which for Weber is not necessarily a mark against it). Although Weber became most famous for his analysis of institutions and bureaucracy in terms of "rationality," he himself was an ethical non-cognitivist and saw rationality and rationalization in terms of a costly "disenchantment" with the world. At the end of his famous book on *The Protestant Ethic and the Spirit of Capitalism* he argued that rationalism is destructive of value, an "iron cage" in which both freedom and meaning are sacrificed to efficiency.[13] One should not be surprised, therefore, that charisma came to offer a significantly religious promise for him.[14]

I may or may not have made my point, but I now want to take a more measured view of charisma. Without identifying it as an attribute of emotional integrity (again, evil leaders may be loaded with it) I think I can allow that charisma *may be* the direct product of emotional integrity. This has the decided dual advantage of taking the mystery out of charisma while at the same time explaining the difficulty with saying just what charisma is. It is not just a single feature, much less a mysterious feature like an "aura," but a complex meta-emotional aspect of a leader's character that requires a suitably complex analysis of his or her emotions and their expression and the way these emotions all tie together. Thus we may be able to transcend James MacGregor Burns' warning that the "term [charisma] is so overused it threatens to collapse under close analysis."[15] At least in a great many praiseworthy cases, charisma may be nothing more than emotional integrity. It helps us understand why Bernard Bass describes charisma as displayed by leaders "to whom followers form deep emotional attachments and who in turn inspire their followers to transcend their own interests for super-ordinate goals."[16] When C. Hodgkinson warns, "Beware charisma,"[17] and Michael Keeley, in a powerful essay, attacks "transformational leadership" precisely on the grounds that it gives too much credence to charisma and too little to the Madisonian "checks and balances" that control or contain charisma,[18] we may be able to respond that charisma *without* emotional integrity may indeed be dangerous, and that emotional integrity carries with it its own "checks and balances" (though more Aristotelian than Madisonian).

Weber celebrated charisma precisely for its spontaneity and freedom, its sense of "sovereignty" that was so at odds with institutions and rational methods. He opposed "charismatic" authority to "rational–legal" and "traditional" authority, where the former is the paradigm of institutions, the latter rather the paradigm of communities and more "natural" organizations.[19] Compared to "rational–legal" authority, charismatic leadership was "irrational," and there can be little doubt that such was the quality that drew Weber – as so many of his German predecessors and successors – to it. Yet he himself rejected the things that could not be analyzed, the overly poetic, and the romantic. I think (and have argued at length) that Weber (like many of his contemporaries) grossly overstated the opposition between rationality and our emotional lives (thus understood as "irrational"). I think that what Weber was actually trying to understand was the ways in which our emotions can be integrated to provide their own form of rationality, a passionate rationality, if you like, or what I have been calling emotional integrity.

EMOTIONAL INTEGRITY AND TRUST

At the core of any discussion of emotional integrity and leadership is the relationship between the leader and the led, and, in particular, the relationship of trust. The word "trust" appears in virtually every book on leadership. It is taken as a commonplace that without trust, leadership is impossible. It is not just the fact that followers trust the leader, because that puts all of the emphasis on the emotions of the followers and not on those of the leader. One might say that the leader should be trustworthy, and thus worthy of his or her followers' trust. But this, I think, is a misunderstanding of the situation. It is trust, that is, the emotional nature of *trusting*, that is important here, over and above the desire that the leader be trustworthy.

Several standard definitions of trust (for example N. Luhmann, B. Barber) characterize it primarily in terms of *expectations*,[20] but this is only half of the story. Trust also involves decisions and the dynamics of a relationship. Trust involves self-confidence and a judicious balance between suspicion and trust and, no doubt, other emotions too. Trust entails not only taking a risk but also a "leap of faith," and this involves all of those emotions having to do with courage, possibly friendship, and good management as well. Trust involves such emotions and requires having them in a holistic way that allows for considerable flexibility coupled with keen ethical judgment. It is about more than "taking a chance," or liking the other person. It has everything to do with the character of the person who trusts and only secondarily the trustworthiness of the person trusted. Trust, in other words, is an essential aspect of emotional integrity.

Niklas Luhmann distinguishes trust from confidence, noting that we trust (or don't trust) people but have (or do not have) confidence in institutions. I think this points to an important distinction, but it does not yet reach it. The distinction between persons and organizations is convenient and obvious but often, especially in business and organizational ethics, misleading or counter-productive. Organizations and institutions have many features of persons (not least, that in the eye of the law they are persons, with fiduciary obligations, rights, and responsibilities). On the one hand, we trust them (or not), much as we would trust a person who had made us a promise or with whom we had agreed upon a contract. On the other hand, we sometimes have confidence in people we do not or would not trust, for example, bureaucrats who are known for their fairness and efficiency but are personally unknown to us. We may also have confidence in someone precisely because we do not trust them, for instance, when we place our confidence in the double-dealing habits of an old and well-known enemy, or "have confidence" that our friend M will fail to quit smoking this time as he has every one of the last thirty-one attempts to do so. (This use of "have confidence" is not wholly ironic.)

Trust is an umbrella term. It is not an emotion as such, although in certain situations it can manifest itself as a very powerful emotion, notably and most dramatically in the case of betrayal, but also in its positive display. One way of describing this feature of trust is to say that, by its very nature, it is part of the "background" of our social activities.[21] To say that trust is not as such an emotion is not, however, to remove it from the realm of emotion – quite the contrary. Trust is the framework within which emotions appear, their precondition, the structure of the world in which they operate. Thus it may be identical with emotional integrity rather than simply an aspect of it.

Without trust, there can be no betrayal, but, more generally, without trust, there can be no cooperation, no community, no commerce, no conversation.[22] In a context without trust, of course, all sorts of emotions readily surface, starting with suspicion and quickly escalating to contempt, resentment, hatred, and worse. Thus "trust" serves to characterize an entire network of emotions and emotional attitudes, both between individuals and within groups and by way of a psychodynamic profile of entire societies. In such large contexts, one might even say that trust is something of an "atmosphere," a shared emotional understanding about who is or who is not to be included, contracted, "trusted." Without trust, there can be no emotional integrity, because the emotions that are to be integrated will be overwhelmed if not eliminated by distrust and the fear of betrayal, perhaps even paranoia.

It is all too common to think of trust in negative terms, for example, as a suspension of fear or a suspension of certain thoughts. While this captures an important insight (namely, that trust as such doesn't *feel* like anything in particular), it fails to capture the important positive dimensions of trust because of a much more general failure to appreciate the nature and character of emotion. Put one way, perhaps too starkly, emotions are not feelings, except in the most generic and, for the most part, vacuous sense of that term (as any felt mental state or experience). Emotions are a systematic set of judgments, and trust, by way of this perspective, is a certain *conception* of the world and other people. It is a way of seeing, a way of estimating and valuing. Trust establishes a framework of expectations and agreements (explicit or not) in which actions conform or fail to conform. A good leader, one might surmise, is one who succeeds in establishing or sustaining a framework of trust, but this begins with cultivating his or her own sense of trust. Indeed, leaders have the primary responsibility for establishing a framework of trust, and this in turn means that they have the responsibility to cultivate trust in themselves.

The emotional dimension of trust involves an active relationship. This is most evident when trust is most in question, for example, at the negotiating table with two bitter and mutually wholly distrustful enemies. Here is where leadership brings emotional integrity to the dramatic forefront. Bill Clinton's sincere efforts to resolve the Israeli–Palestinian and (more successfully) the

Northern Ireland crises are exemplary, in this regard, whatever one might think of other aspects of Clinton's emotional character in more personal domains. It was his dedication to bringing peace – whether or not he also thought of it in terms of his personal reputation and place in history – that had such an effect not only on the participants but on the entire region. Trust does not reside in a single all-or-nothing decision but rather in persistence and incremental increases, and it may take a particularly positive and perseverant mediator to broker such trust.

What seems to have gotten lost is the idea that trust is not only something that must be *earned,* but what is more important is that trust is something to be had, something to be *given.* Giving trust is a dynamic decision, the transformation of the most basic and sometimes most difficult kind. This, I would suggest, is central to any conception of "transforming" or "transformational leadership," indeed, to any leadership at all. But this places an enormous burden of leadership, perhaps ironically, on the led. It is their decision, to trust or not to trust, that makes leadership possible, and much of the traditional talk about charisma as "a special quality," I would suggest, might better be viewed as the endowment or the projection of such a property, by way of the people who then "find" that property worthy of following. But whether or not trust can be earned, it can be wisely or foolishly given. This is why the emotional integrity of those who would follow, not only of those who would lead, is fundamental to good leadership.

NOTES

1. Many thanks to Joanne Ciulla for her helpful comments (and prompting).
2. Antonio Damasio, *Descartes Error: Emotion, Reason, and the Human Brain,* New York: Avon Books, 1994. In declaring that "Leadership is all about people's emotions" I do not mean to short-change rationality, but what Damasio has shown and I have long argued is that emotions and rationality are not antagonists but mostly cooperative partners, at least in healthy people.
3. Niccolò Machiavelli, *The Prince,* trans. Christian E. Detmold, New York: Airmont, 1965.
4. Robert C. Solomon, *The Passions,* New York: Doubleday, 1976, and *Not Passion's Slave,* New York: Oxford University Press, 2003.
5. Damasio, 1994.
6. Robert C. Solomon, *A Better Way to Think About Business,* New York, Oxford University Press, 1999.
7. Soren Kierkegaard, *The Present Age,* New York, Oxford University Press, 1962; Nietzsche, *On the Genealogy of Morals,* New York, Random House, 1967.
8. This distinction between following and "making one's own" is the central tenet of many existentialist philosophies. The nineteenth century Danish philosopher Soren Kierkegaard thus distinguished between "Christendom," which involves unthinking obedience to Christian beliefs and values, and truly becoming a Christian, which involves a passionate personal commitment. So, too, more recently Martin Heidegger in Germany and Jean-Paul Sartre in France insisted on "resolution" and "authenticity" rather than mere rule-following.

And although none of them use the word as we do, one might well summarize this aspect of their philosophies by calling it "integrity."

9. Friedrich Nietzsche, *Beyond Good and Evil*, New York: Random House, 1966.
10. Quoted in Jill Lawrence, "Attacked on defense Issues: Kerry Fires Back," *USA Today*, 4/28/04, p. A6.
11. Daniel Goleman, *Emotional Intelligence*, New York: Bantam Books, 1995.
12. Robert C. Solomon, "Ethical Leadership, Emotions, and Trust: Beyond Charisma," in Joanne B. Ciulla (ed.), *Ethics, The Heart of Leadership*, Westport, CT: Praeger, 1998.
13. Max Weber, *The Protestant Ethic and the Spirit of Capitalism*, trans. by Talcott Parsons, New York: Scribners, 1958.
14. Max Weber, "The Sociology of Charismatic Authority" in Gerth and Mills (eds), *From Max Weber*, Oxford, Oxford University Press, 1946, pp. 245ff. The Weberian term is defined by the *American Heritage Dictionary* as: 1.a. A rare personal quality attributed to leaders who arouse fervent popular devotion and enthusiasm. b. Personal magnetism or charm. 2. Theology. An extraordinary power, such as the ability to perform miracles, granted to a Christian by the Holy Spirit.
15. James MacGregor Burns, *Leadership*, New York: Harper, 1978, p. 243.
16. Bernard M. Bass, *Leadership and Performance Beyond Expectations*, New York: Free Press, 1985.
17. Quoted by Edwin P. Hollander, "Ethical Challenges in the Leader–Follower Relationship," in Ciulla, 1998, p. 57.
18. Michael, Keeley, "The Trouble with Transformational Leadership," in Ciulla, 1998.
19. Max Weber, *Theory of Social and Economic Organization*, trans. by A. Henderson and T. Parsons, New York, Free Press, 1947.
20. See, Niklas Luhmann, in Tom Burns, Gianfranco Poggi (ed.), *Trust and Power*, trans. by Howard Davis, John Raffan and Kathryn Rooney, Chichester, NY: Wiley, 1979, p. 80; and Bernard Barber, *Logic and Limits of Trust*, New Brunswick, NJ: Rutgers University Press, 1983, pp. 2, 71.
21. The concept of the "background" comes from Heidegger and his analyses of human practices in general, but it is also explained in a more analytic framework by John Searle in his book, *Intentionality*, New York: Cambridge University Press, 1983.
22. Of course, there can be banter and all kind of "speech," but the number of "speech acts" that simply break down is mind-boggling, and not only those that depend on trust that the other person is telling the truth.

3. Ethical diversity and the leader's religious commitments

Douglas A. Hicks

INTRODUCTION

Contrary to popular portrayals of leadership that create a too-simple dichotomy between ethical and unethical leadership, the determination of what, precisely, is ethical leadership behavior is the real challenge. The complex realities of organizations and societies require substantive and contested debate even when all parties agree that they want their leaders to be ethical and to act ethically. Disagreements among diverse schools of Western philosophical thought – for example, virtue ethics, deontology, consequentialism – complicate the question of what is ethical.

In addition to philosophical ideas, multiple religious traditions provide and shape ethical schools of thought. One need not look far on the shelves of popular leadership literature to see that advocates and adherents of servant leadership, for instance, cite the example of Jesus as the paradigm of the leader who came not to be served, but to serve.[1] Various analysts have put forth their own theological–ethical approaches or critiques of leadership from a Christian perspective.[2] References to religious sources of morality reach beyond Christianity to other religions. Robert Greenleaf's account of the servant as leader, while deeply influenced by Christian ideas, also relates his notion to Eastern mystic traditions.[3] One of the most notable demographic trends of the past four decades – in the US as well as in many parts of the "globalizing" world – is the multiplication of religious backgrounds, worldviews, and practices among the citizenry. As one consequence of this broadening, the spirituality and leadership literature now includes perspectives from fundamentalist and conservative Christianity, mainline and liberal Protestant Christianity, Catholic and Orthodox spirituality, Jewish (from orthodox to reform to mystical), Muslim, Buddhist, Hindu, Taoist, Native American, New Age religion, and generically spiritual traditions.[4]

The central question of this chapter is: given the ethical diversity of public settings – whether corporate, non-profit, or governmental – how should the leader draw upon his or her religious faith as a source of ethical ideas and actions? As I have suggested, this question is just one part of the wider question concerning how a leader should draw upon her or his own worldview and values in leading a group of persons who do not embrace all (or perhaps any) of those commitments. If religion and religious difference were somehow absent from a contemporary workplace, organization, or society, ethical differences would still exist and could potentially create tensions. Yet, for a variety of reasons, leadership scholars tend to treat religious commitments as particularly divisive or problematic. These reasons relate to the so-called secularization of the public spheres of business, social service, and government and hence the apparent relegation of religion to a private or domestic sphere; the sheer complexity and variety of religious beliefs and practices; and recent attempts to reduce multiple, particular religious ideas to a generic spirituality that might more easily connect to secular values.[5]

This chapter examines the distinctive problems that the positional leader – in contrast to followers – faces when she adheres to her religious convictions in diverse organizations. Drawing upon a framework of respectful pluralism, the chapter argues that the leader's position of influence – potential power over followers, intended or unintended – creates unique challenges for the leader. Her position requires balancing the exercise of her own religious commitments with efforts to develop a respectful environment that invites the open expression by followers of their religiously based and other ethical commitments. This instance of a special responsibility or burden is not unlike other challenges unique to leaders. Leaders think their situation is special – and it is – and the ethical challenge for leaders (in concert with their followers) is to determine the exceptions as well as distinctive responsibilities they should properly accept for themselves.[6] This chapter ends with an analysis of one high-profile political leader – US President George W. Bush – and an evaluation of the ways in which he has articulated his religious faith within a diverse US citizenry.

RESPECTFUL PLURALISM AND THE ROLE OF THE LEADER

Elsewhere I have developed a framework of respectful pluralism that can help leaders and followers negotiate religiously based and other forms of diversity in the workplace.[7] With some modifications that take into account contextual factors and different stakeholders, the approach can be applied to other diverse, public leadership settings as well.

The framework of respectful pluralism seeks to steer carefully between a view that prohibits leaders' and followers' religious expression (including ethical reflection alongside other kinds of expression), on the one hand, and one that would allow leaders unduly to influence the religious convictions of their followers. The approach pays particular attention to religious and other forms of diversity, identifying as a central challenge for ethical and effective leadership the wide variety of worldviews present in a public setting such as the workplace and the political sphere.

Respectful pluralism builds upon a *presumption of inclusion* that welcomes into diverse, public settings fundamental aspects of each person's identity. Note that this presumption is quite different from beginning with the view of religion or other "personal" characteristics as somehow unwelcome in public settings. On the contrary, this perspective begins with the view that a person's commitments cut across private and public spheres. This inclusion is constrained, however, by three limiting norms. More precisely stated, to the greatest extent, in public contexts marked by demographic diversity, leaders and followers should be free to express their religious, spiritual, cultural, political, and other commitments, subject to the limiting norms of *noncoercion*, *nondegradation*, and *nonestablishment*, and in consideration of reasonable instrumental demands of the leadership process. *Nondegradation* prohibits words or actions (whether religiously based or not) that have the effect of demeaning a fellow leader or follower or group of followers. *Noncoercion* disallows the use of positional or other forms of power by leaders or colleagues to impose their particular religious, spiritual, cultural, political, or other views or practices on others. Finally, *nonestablishment* requires that no "comprehensive vision of the good" (to borrow a Rawlsian phrase[8]) – whether religious, philosophical, or moral – be adopted or promoted as the official worldview of the diverse, public group. Rather, leaders should shape a "thinner" values-based culture of respect and open communication of differences within their organization, community, or society.[9]

In respectful pluralism, the dignity of each person in the organization is a fundamental moral starting point. It is important to acknowledge that this framework, as all others, depends upon particular ethical assumptions. The fundamental role of dignity and equal respect due each person, however, is embraced in some way by the major Western philosophical traditions and thus is capable of a rather broad consensus. It is, likewise, consistent with some but not all religious and theological accounts. It would not be compatible, however, with any ethical perspective – whether religiously based, philosophically based, or otherwise – that considers gender, race, or sexual orientation as reason for privilege or discrimination. This is no small caveat, and it makes clear that respectful pluralism, though thin, is a particular moral view.

In this framework, no organization or free society should properly require that religious or other forms of commitment that reflect the very identity of a person be excluded from its setting. As long as persons can uphold the constraints created by the norms *nondegradation, noncoercion,* and *nonestablishment,* religious and other expression should be allowed. These limiting norms, of course, have the effect of excluding various kinds of speech and behavior, including those that are religiously based. But they do not exclude because of the religious nature of the speech or actions.

Leaders, like followers, are considered within respectful pluralism as persons with dignity, for whom equal respect demands that they can also draw upon their religious commitments in their participation in the leadership process. These persons in positions of authority or influence, however, play a distinct role in the framework. Although they enjoy the same presumption of inclusion and must uphold the same three limiting norms as followers, their very position dictates that the limiting norms will affect them differently than the norms affect their followers.

Specifically, by definition, persons in a position of influence are more able than others to coerce or degrade others or to institutionalize their individual religious beliefs or practices. It is precisely the fact of being a leader that makes persons more likely to run into the limiting norms.[10] When an employee asks a co-worker to run an errand during lunch break, it seems possible to decline the request; when a boss makes the request, it is less simple to say no. The same goes for asking a colleague to attend a workplace (or church) bible study or requesting participation in a prayer before a staff meeting. In all such cases, the positional leader's touch is heavier than the follower's.[11]

Notice that these norms do not depend upon the intention of the leader. The well-intentioned leader might wish neither to put subordinates in a difficult position to say no nor to impose his or her views on others. Alternatively, some leaders do openly report that they have a responsibility to utilize their position to share a religious message.[12] The relevant factor is the perceived and actual effect from behavior upon subordinates. To be sure, open communication about perceived conflicts of worldviews and values should mark an organization enacting respectful pluralism; subordinates would ideally be able to name religious and other expressions that make them uncomfortable or unduly burdened. Yet, even the ability to name an objection to another's religious expression is constrained by one's position and status within the leadership structure.

Thus, the leader should be able to express his or her religious commitments, but the constraints imposed by the limiting norms make such expression a more complex and potentially problematic challenge for leaders than followers. The analysis of positional power should be undertaken before leaders employ their religious and other commitments – that is, this is part of introspective (as well as other types of environmental and interpersonal) exploration that should take place before they begin to lead at all.

At the same time, the leader has an additional distinctive leadership role: he or she has a responsibility to help create a culture that models respectful pluralism. Leadership scholars have emphasized that effective leaders not only read or understand the culture of their organization, they also help to interpret and shape it for their followers.[13] This is particularly true in creating an environment that is ethical.[14] Even as leaders should have space to express their own religion, they must also send the clear message to their followers that all people are welcome to express their faith (or no faith). This act of culture-shaping is highly dependent upon context (even before that context is influenced by a leader). Does the leader encourage perspectives different from her own – even in conflict with her own – by followers? Is the schedule or calendar of the organization or society shaped to favor, directly or indirectly, adherents of one particular religion? Are adherents of minority traditions adequately and respectfully accommodated? Are there informal opportunities for various persons to share their own background and identity with colleagues on an equal basis? These are the sorts of questions that can help a leader to shape a culture of genuine respect.[15]

The sections below explore further the difficulties of holding in appropriate tension these two goods – a leader's own expression of her identity and a leader's work to create conditions for all to express their identity.

THE LEADER'S RELIGIOUS EXPRESSION: ALTERNATIVES TO RESPECTFUL PLURALISM

Before proceeding further, it is important to examine how the framework of respectful pluralism differs from other possible understandings of a leader's expression of her religious faith. A brief argument for why each of these alternative approaches should be rejected is also offered.

At one end of possible approaches, an organization or society can operate as a hostile context for anyone to express any religious views; a setting or sphere can be declared, in one way or another, a "religion-free zone." This is an extreme form of secularism, in which religion simply is not welcome in whatever form within that context. No one, including those in positional power, can express their religion in an explicit way. In this approach, then, the leader is not treated as special. Any values-laden or ethical discussion is framed in secular philosophical terms. This predominant and "modern" point of view fails to recognize the fundamental relationship between identity and religious expression; the argument from human dignity rejects this simple discounting of religion.[16]

A Marxist variant of this secularist framework allows followers, as persons without much positional influence, to express their religion as they see fit. In this view, religion can be a form of opiate that serves to pacify the followers with their lot. Persons with influence, however, are forbidden to draw upon religion precisely because religion should generally be kept from mixing with "secular" powers. This position takes with full seriousness the concern noted above of potential undue influence of a leader's religious expression to degrade or coerce others, but it fails to acknowledge that the identity, and hence dignity, of leaders as well as others must be respected. Once religion – unlike in the Marxist view – is treated as a not necessarily misguided aspect of identity, some form of balancing of potentially competing values must take place.

A third kind of approach to (not) allowing the leader's religious expression involves constructing a form of faith or spirituality that is peculiar to the public setting itself and that can be shared by persons from multiple religious affiliations. In the political sphere, this approach has resulted in various forms of civil religion – a religious or quasi-religious expression of the state, in which the "congregation" becomes the nation's entire citizenry.[17] In workplace contexts, many practitioners and writers have proposed a common spirituality (or what I call a generic spirituality) that unites workers regardless of their more "rigid" or "dogmatic" religious views. In the case of civil religion as well as generic spirituality, the leader opts to appeal to quasi-religious ideas of the unified collective instead of deliberate or particular reference to one's own religious tradition. In the US political context, most presidents have referred, in their formal addresses, to some Christian and (to a lesser extent) Jewish symbols and images while appropriating them to affirm a faith in America itself.[18] Civil religion is examined in more detail below. In general terms, civil religion and generic spirituality tend to deny the particularity and differences across religious traditions in a simple quest for unity, even as they give some indirect preference to the religion of the majority, from which many of the so-called generic symbols derive. Further, faith in country or faith in a company, for instance, makes ethical demands that can clash with genuine religious commitments of citizens and employees, respectively. Civil religion and generic spirituality, however, tend to downplay these potential commitment clashes by favoring nation or workplace over religious commitment. Such commitment clashes include those that leaders themselves potentially face – for example, on whether to send a nation to war or on whether to produce a potentially harmful product.

Each of the perspectives discussed thus far tends to deny religious expression of leaders while rightly emphasizing the importance of not unduly influencing followers. The class of frameworks, below, does the opposite. This type of approach invites or encourages leaders to share their religion while improperly minimizing the potentially inappropriate effects on others.

Approaches that emphasize "faith at work" or connecting religion and public life often assume both a commonality of religious expression among all participants in a leadership process and a necessary connection between religion and morality. To be specific, in the US context, analysts frequently conflate the terms religious, Christian, and ethical,[19] paying little attention to non-Christian religious or ethical traditions. This approach is distinct from the generic spirituality approach, because the former does not reduce or translate particular religious commitments into generic ones. On the contrary, it involves an attempt to understand the public sphere and its values in Christian terms. In this frame, the Christian leader often has the moral (and theological) duty to employ his position to further God's kingdom. While approaches vary from encouraging respect (or at least polite tolerance) for followers of other religions to outright disdain for non-Christian approaches to morality, all assume a rather direct application of the Christian principles of the leader into the public values of the organization or public sphere. These approaches, in which Christian leaders "Christianize" their public leadership context, fail to uphold respect for non-Christians. If a public context permits religious expression by Christians, it should do so on the grounds of equal respect – by permitting adherents of other religions to express their faith publicly as well.

In addition, the norm of non-establishment disallows any religious expression that would become, *de jure* or *de facto*, an official practice or policy of the workplace or state. This critical distinction between individual religious expression, on one hand, and official organizational or governmental expression, on the other, is admittedly difficult, especially for leaders, whose actions are often seen as representative or official – whether or not they intend them to be. Let us turn to explore the potential conflicts of individual and institutional religion in the case of one high-profile leader.

PERSONAL RELIGION AND A PLURALISTIC CULTURE: THE CASE OF GEORGE W. BUSH

As a way of applying the framework of respectful pluralism to understand the beliefs and actions of a given leader, this section offers a constructive and critical analysis of a topic that has received much public attention of late: George W. Bush's religious expression in his role as President of the United States. For the purposes of this examination, this chapter's guiding question can be applied as follows: given the ethical diversity of the United States citizenry, how should the president appropriately draw upon his religious faith as a source of ethical ideas and actions?

Commentators have written a great deal about the faith of President George W. Bush.[20] He has discussed it publicly himself in his autobiography, and its very title, *A Charge to Keep*, reflects his Methodist, Christian faith.[21] Bush brought his religion directly into the campaign in 2000 when he answered a question, in a presidential debate, with the claim that the most influential political philosopher in his life has been "Christ, because he changed my heart."[22] His 2004 campaign, including responses given in the presidential debates, reiterated the importance he places on his Christian faith. In major speeches, radio addresses, declarations, and press conferences, Bush has referred to God and God's purposes, and especially America's role in bringing about God's designs for the world as well as God's plan for America as a kind of divine instrument.

Robert Bellah's seminal 1967 analysis of civil religion in America sets a precedent for analyzing how presidents have employed religious themes in their public addresses.[23] Notwithstanding the intellectual debates spawned by his article, Bellah convincingly demonstrates how most (if not all) US presidents, particularly in modern times, have opted to describe and promote a religion (or quasi-religion) of the nation in lieu of a specific account of Christianity. Hence for most presidents there is far more emphasis on notions of a providential God and general morality than there are references to a God in Trinitarian form or to Jesus Christ. Presidential speeches make ample reference to a God who blesses America and who provides its citizens with freedom, justice, and equality. In this civil religion, Americans who serve their country also in some way work for God's purposes.

The major addresses and declarations of George W. Bush display a president who regularly embraces the themes of American civil religion. In his 2001 Inaugural address Bush appealed to the story of America, paying particular heed to "this story's author, who fills time and eternity with his purpose. Yet his purpose is achieved in our duty, and our duty is fulfilled in service to one another."[24] Bush concluded his 2003 State of the Union address with these words:

> We Americans have faith in ourselves, but not in ourselves alone. We do not claim to know all of the ways of Providence, yet we can trust in them, placing our confidence in the loving God behind all of life and all of history. May he guide us now, and may God continue to bless the United States of America.[25]

While these and other examples occur in high-profile addresses, references to providence, the Almighty, and human duty to the Creator appear frequently in his various speeches.

Bush and his speechwriters often cite the ways in which Washington, Jefferson, Lincoln, Franklin Roosevelt, and other presidents appealed to divine providence in their declarations. In this way, Bush stakes a claim to the tradition of American civil religion. Critics of civil religion also see Bush as a too-eager adherent to this tradition, particularly as he has employed it to bolster patriotism in a time of international conflict.[26]

At the same time, Bush's references to his own *Christian* faith (beyond his mere upholding of *American* civic faith) come through in many of his declarations and speeches. To a degree beyond that of any other president in the modern era, particularly the post-1965 era of renewed immigration and widening religious diversity in the US, Bush imbues his speeches with references to Christian scriptures (and even hymns). Many of these examples move him beyond the standard claims to American civil religion to make more direct appeals to Christianity. His post-September 11, 2001 address in the National Cathedral[27] included a direct citation of a Christian New Testament passage, Romans 8:38–9, with a suggestion that all citizens would know the text:

> As we've been assured, neither death, nor life, nor angels, nor principalities, nor powers, nor things present, nor things to come, nor height, nor depth, can separate us from God's love.[28]

In his Inaugural address Bush referred to Jesus' parable of the "good Samaritan" (Luke 10:29–37), not only as a story that all Americans were expected to know, but as a normative vision for the country: "And I can pledge our nation to a goal: When we see that wounded traveler on the road to Jericho, we will not pass to the other side."[29]

The tradition of American civil religion has long drawn general theological concepts from Christianity, including ideas taken from the Hebrew scriptures shared with Judaism. Presidents before Bush have made references to Christian biblical passages in their official speeches. Yet, Bush's frequency and specificity of scriptural citation is arguably more frequent and specific than that of any other president of the modern era.

Even as the president has made his understanding of Christian faith highly public, George W. Bush has continued earlier presidents' efforts[30] to expand his reference to religious persons and communities beyond Christians and Jews as fully part of America. Bush has regularly referred in major speeches to Muslims, mosques, and the crescent of Islam, including in his Inaugural address and his 2004 State of the Union address.[31] Within a week after the terrorist attacks in the US on September 11, 2001, Bush made a high-profile visit to the Islamic Center of Greater Washington.[32] A few days earlier, Bush had been widely criticized for his earlier remarks that called the war on terrorism a "crusade," a statement that his own advisers later acknowledged was an unfortunate reference to centuries of predominantly Christian-upon-Muslim violence.[33]

In his remarks on religious freedom, Bush has consistently stated his view that America is a place that welcomes persons regardless of their religion. This is not to say, however, that he has been free from criticism in terms of (not) acknowledging the diverse religions of the citizenry. Some analysts note that he has only occasionally referred to citizens outside of the Abrahamic (that is, Christian, Jewish, Islamic) traditions.[34]

Other critics have maintained that, more than what traditions or persons Bush lists when referring to religious diversity, Bush's inclusion of selected non-Christian traditions fits only within his Christian-defined understanding of what, precisely, religion is. That is, even the notion of "religion as faith" – which has influenced his "Faith-Based Initiative" – is a predominantly Protestant, Christian view not held by persons of other traditions. That is, as opposed to most strands of Christian Protestantism, in which faith or a set of beliefs is most significant, for many traditions (for example, Judaism, Hinduism, Native American traditions), rituals or practices, and not beliefs, are most central.[35] In other words, if non-Christian traditions are welcomed in George W. Bush's Faith-Based Initiative or, more generally, in the American environment he is shaping through his leadership, it is not on a "level playing field" with Christianity. Rather, extending the metaphor, citizens of non-Christian religions may express their religion on what is Christianity's home field.

From a perspective of respectful pluralism, it is important to ask whether and how Bush has managed to balance expressing his own religious identity with creating a culture of equal respect for persons of all religious backgrounds. In the current context of religious diversity in the US, have Bush's prolific references to his own faith, to Christian scripture, and to the importance of prayer had a cumulative effect – sending a message to non-Christians that they are not as welcome or included as American citizens as their Christian counterparts are? Posing the question in this way does not answer it. It encourages citizens to discuss further the ways in which religious identity of a leader should properly interrelate with the religious freedom and identity of followers.

In respectful pluralism, the limiting norms of *nondegradation, noncoercion*, and *nonestablishment* are standards for considering this question. As noted in an earlier section, the question of a leader's (that is, the president's) intention is not a directly relevant factor in employing these norms. Do non-Christian citizens (or other Christians, for that matter) experience degradation from Bush's public references to his own faith or to Christianity in general? It is reasonable to conclude that none of Bush's statements cited above (with the probable exception of his use of the term "crusade," which was admitted to be a mistake and corrected) have had the direct effect of degrading persons of non-Christian backgrounds. A more complicated case for less-than-full inclusion for non-Christians, however, might be made along lines of nondegradation. That is, the repeated reference to Christian scripture in his speeches and the frequent outreach to religious leaders arguably makes persons from non-Christian traditions feel like outsiders or as second-class citizens. In reply to this criticism, the president and his proponents would cite his by-now multiple visits to Islamic Centers, his multi-religious holiday declarations, and his inclusion of multiple religions in prayer breakfasts and the like. As discussed above, his critics counter that these nods at inclusion leave the basic Christian ethos and assumptions of the events unchanged.

The case of the limiting norm of *noncoercion* can similarly be analyzed in two parts, along the lines of direct coercion and indirect coercion. Bush has been clear in defending freedom of religious expression, even for persons of no religious background. The cases (at least those discussed herein) do not indicate any directly coercive uses of religion by the president. More convincing arguments that Bush has been coercive focus less on Bush's words in his public pronouncements and more on his promotion of his faith-based initiative and his moral stands on issues like marriage and abortion that he attributes rather directly to his own "compassionate-conservative" Christianity. Opponents of aid to faith-based social-service agencies and defenders of abortion rights have strongly denounced Bush's appeals to faith as coercive to the rights of citizens.[36] It is worth noting here that some persons who believe this use of religion is coercive are Christians who disagree with Bush either on the view of Christianity or on his view on the degree of directness of the relationship between religious ideas and the political order.

Analysts have various reasons to criticize President Bush for the appearance of showing favoritism to evangelical Christians. The US Attorney General of his first administration, John Ashcroft, brought a high-profile Christian faith into the office charged with defending religious and other civil rights, when the civil liberties of Muslim Americans were under fire. In addition, Bush made frequent appearances before evangelical groups, including the Southern Baptist Convention, and the 2000 and 2004 campaigns made other overtures to evangelicals that gave credence to the view that evangelicals had special access to the White House.

The third limiting norm, *nonestablishment*, focuses on the degree to which the religion of an individual leader becomes, *de facto* at least, a religion of the institution. In this case, to what degree do faith-based statements or actions by George W. Bush, while he is president, appear to be official (for example governmentally endorsed) statements or actions? Analysis along this vein opens up many questions about the relationship between Christianity and official state roles and functions – a thicket largely beyond the scope of this chapter. Yet, the question of to what extent religiously based declarations by the president of the United States appear to be official endorsements of those religious views remains a pressing one. Frequent and specific reference to Christian scriptures in official declarations does not amount to legal establishment of Christianity, but they do raise serious concerns about a cultural privileging of that religion over others in relation to state power.

An issue related to the second and third limiting norms is the degree of closeness between the religious faith of a leader and his moral justifications for a policy or public action. Does Bush as president of the United States make improperly theological justifications for his moral stances on positions, such as marriage, abortion, and war? The framework of respectful pluralism clearly includes space for a president (as well as any other leader or citizen) to hold deep and sincere theological, religious, and other beliefs about important issues. The leader has not only a right, but an obligation to communicate those convictions in some way with his followers. At the same time, the other aspect of respectful pluralism, the one that grounds the limiting norms, is the message sent to followers in terms of their own moral and religious convictions. According to the norm of *nonestablishment*, the president should be careful to separate his own deepest commitments from the lawmaking process or the enforcement of existing laws. And, in this case, the First Amendment prohibits any legal establishment of theological or religious principles.

How, then, should a president rightly appeal to his or her theological convictions? The late political and moral philosopher John Rawls suggested a framework of public reason, by which leaders communicate to their citizens in terms that demonstrate civility and mutual respect for all citizens regardless of their religious or non-religious background. This language and its justificatory terms are necessarily non-religious (and also not exclusive to any philosophical or moral traditions that offer a "comprehensive vision of the good").[37] In his revised, expanded view of public reason, Rawls allows leaders to appeal to their religious convictions, as long as they tie them directly to secular, public values (for example, liberty, equality, justice) that all citizens can understand.[38] The framework of respectful pluralism, more so than Rawls's frame, includes hope that persons across religious (and philosophical, cultural, political) differences can find ways – in their own terms – to communicate with each other. Thus, respectful pluralism offers more space than Rawls's frame does for a president to communicate the relationship between his faith or other commitments and the moral and policy implications of those commitments.

President Bush's frequent reference to a "culture of life" – with respect to his anti-abortion-rights position and other moral–political issues, has its roots in his own faith and, in particular, the language of the Roman Catholic Church. Pope John Paul II built his moral theology around his account of the gospel of life, even labeling one of his major encyclicals with this title.[39] Bush reports being highly influenced by Richard John Neuhaus's use of this term in his own decision to adopt the language of a "culture of life," specifically in relation to the question of abortion.[40]

In general terms, respectful pluralism tempers the excessive influence of a leader's religious commitments in various ways, such as: through limited frequency, through clarification about one's own personal convictions in contrast to national policies, and through explicit invitation to voices from other traditions also to be highly visible and public in their articulation of morality. Rather than dictate a formula for how and when to communicate one's religion, however, the framework of respectful pluralism merely provides guidelines and questions, along the lines considered above, of how to guarantee the leader's identity while also attending to a culture of respect and welcome for all religious and other moral perspectives.

CONCLUSIONS

The examination of President George W. Bush's religious convictions and his public role as leader serves to highlight the myriad challenges of mixing public life and religion, and of balancing commitments between religious and political roles. This closing section states some conclusions from the analysis of this case, bringing to bear the insights of the earlier discussions of ethical diversity and the leader's religious convictions. The potential ways in which the frame of respectful pluralism can help to navigate these challenges are highlighted.

The analysis of Bush's employment of religious language, symbols, and ideas describes a leader who sees a rather direct, even uncomplicated, application of his personal faith to leadership of a diverse nation. When asked, in April 2000, to explain what he meant when he said that his most influential political philosopher was "Christ, because he changed my heart,"[41] Bush replied that, while it is difficult to explain, believing in Christ changes someone personally, as it had done for him. He declined in this case, as in many others, to acknowledge the complexities involved in drawing upon, applying, or translating the personal religious transformation into acting as a leader within the wider public order. Yet that, after all, is one challenge of political philosophy and of political leadership.

The key ingredient emphasized in the framework of respectful pluralism but that seems to be underplayed in Bush's political leadership is the potentially undue influence of a leader's own religious faith – and ethical convictions – upon a citizenry that is religiously and morally diverse. Although he consistently acknowledges religious difference among Americans in his public addresses, he often quickly moves to claim that a large swath of common ethical convictions is shared by followers of many religions, and by persons of no religion. In this quick dismissal of genuine difference or disagreement on ethical issues, Bush is able to claim that his religious worldview (which is, after all, not so different from others' views) provides moral grounding for his – that is, the executive branch's or the government's – policies or actions.

It is important to take note of the fact that genuine disagreements, even conflicts, exist among persons of very similar religious worldviews. Some of President Bush's strongest critics of his uses of religion are Christian clergy and scholars, including evangelicals.[42] Too frequently, the potentially conflictual role of religion is equated with tensions, say, between Christians and Jews, or between Hindus and Muslims. But ethical and political and other forms of disagreement occur among religious communities as well. Similarly, differences of view occur among groupings by racial-ethnic, gender-based, and other aspects of identity. In brief, as James MacGregor Burns, Ronald Heifetz, and many others have pointed out, political leadership will involve conflicts, and good leadership negotiates, rather than denies, those conflicts.[43] Religion is no different from politics, culture, or economics in this respect, but in order for differences and tensions to be addressed, they must be acknowledged and adjudicated.

When a positional leader, whether president, CEO, or otherwise, draws deeply and directly upon his or her religious convictions, creating an unevenly footed discussion among persons with different moral, spiritual, and religious worldviews, it becomes a leadership problem. The norms of respectful pluralism – and the questions they can spawn for leaders to pose to themselves – can help leaders to be sure that their influence is not excessive or inappropriate. Naming as honestly and openly as one is able to do – including asking for criticism – his or her own moral convictions, and inviting other persons, religious and otherwise, to speak up with no risk of reprisal, are key elements in this task.

But what if a leader is absolutely certain of his or her religious convictions?[44] What if he or she feels morally or theologically compelled to impose those ethical convictions (perhaps with the best of intentions) on a society or its population? After all, some critics of religion do not see that a person of conviction could hold back from imposing their beliefs and practices upon others if they held them to be true. Yet a long tradition of thinkers, particularly but not exclusively in the West, has held, in essence, that religion imposed is no religion at all. From James Madison, Thomas Jefferson, and other American founders, to more recent advocates of religious freedom and disestablishment like John Courtney Murray and Ronald Thiemann, the need to avoid imposition of values upon others has been held paramount.[45] Even more to the point, John Locke argued in his classic 1689 essay that recognizing uncertainty, particularly in matters religious, is a fundamental part of good political leadership. He was especially critical of religious leaders who sought to impose their religious beliefs and practices by establishing an official religion of the nation. In more general terms, it was mandatory for leaders to understand the limitations in their own religious knowledge:

> Now, neither the care of the commonwealth, nor the right of enacting laws, does discover this way that leads to heaven more certainly to the magistrate, than every private man's search and study discovers it unto himself. . . . Princes, indeed, are born superior unto other men in power, but in nature equal. Neither the right, nor

the art of ruling, does necessarily carry along with it the certain knowledge of other things; and least of all true religion.[46]

In a very different context, Terry Price's own cautionary analysis of human's epistemic limits serves to question leaders who fail to acknowledge the fact that they might be mistaken in their religious beliefs.[47]

This focus upon the potential problems posed by leaders who draw significantly upon religious commitments in their public roles does not lead us to the conclusion, however, that leaders must check their convictions and practices at the door when they enter the workplace or the political arena. On the contrary, recall that the framework of respectful pluralism begins with the presumption of inclusion. However, as is evident from this chapter, that inclusion is significantly circumscribed by the special place enjoyed by leaders in the power structure and the leadership process. The leader himself or herself bears significant responsibility for shaping a culture in which communication about religiously based and other moral differences can be raised. Whether in the White House or in lower-profile leadership posts, the positional authority that leaders hold affords them the opportunity – alas, an obligation – to highlight the differences among all participants in the leadership process as well as the potential tensions arising from these differences. Religious convictions may, frequently, be deeply held and diverse among employees or citizens, but like other aspects central to one's personal and moral identity, they do not necessarily lead to unhealthy conflict.

Thus a pivotal leadership challenge concerns not only holding to one's own ethical convictions (whether religiously based or not) but, in addition, helping groups of diverse people to navigate moral differences to arrive together at common leadership ends. The framework of respectful pluralism will need to be applied and adapted to fit each specific context, but its general approach allows leaders to view ethical (even religious) diversity as part of the leadership challenge that can be negotiated constructively.

NOTES

1. The phrase comes from Mark 10:45: "For the Son of Man came not to be served but to serve, to give his life as a ransom for many."
2. One recent work in this area is Bernice Ledbetter and Robert J. Banks, *Reviewing Leadership: A Christian Evaluation of Current Approaches* (Grand Rapids, MI: Baker Academic, 2004).
3. Robert K. Greenleaf, *The Servant as Leader: A Journey into the Nature of Legitimate Power and Greatness* (New York: Paulist Press, 1977), drawing on Hermann Hesse, *Journey to the East* (New York: Farrar, Straus and Giroux, 1976).
4. For a fuller account of the diversity of religion in US society and workplaces, see Douglas A. Hicks, *Religion and the Workplace: Pluralism, Spirituality, Leadership* (Cambridge: Cambridge University Press, 2003), chapters 1 and 2.
5. Hicks, *Religion and the Workplace*, chapters 3 and 4.

6.   Terry L. Price, *Understanding Ethical Failures of Leadership* (Cambridge: Cambridge University Press, 2006).
7.   Hicks, *Religion and the Workplace*, chapters 8 and 9.
8.   John Rawls, *Political Liberalism* (New York: Columbia University Press, 1993).
9.   Hicks, *Religion and the Workplace*, chapters 8 and 9.
10. The likelihood of a leader's conflict with the limiting norms is heightened by the cognitive failures of leadership outlined by Price in *Understanding Ethical Failures of Leadership*. On this view, leaders come to think that the dangers of coercing or degrading followers do not apply to them; why should they have to adhere to the limiting norms?
11. To be sure, a particular follower might have more relational, or referent, power than a given leader. This type of power should also be examined. Indeed, relational powers and positional power can compound the influence that a leader can have over followers.
12. Laura L. Nash, *Believers in Business* (Nashville, TN: Thomas Nelson Publishers, 1994).
13. Edgar H. Schein, *Organizational Culture and Leadership* (2nd edition, San Francisco, CA: Jossey-Bass, 1992); Terrence E. Deal and Allan A. Kennedy, *Corporate Cultures* (Boston, MA: Addison Wesley, 1982).
14. Joanne B. Ciulla, "Messages from the Environment: The Influences of Policies and Practices on Employee Responsibility," in Chimezie A. B. Osigweh, Yg., ed., *Communicating Employee Responsibilities and Rights: A Modern Management Mandate* (New York: Quorum, 1987), pp. 133–40.
15. See Hicks, *Religion and the Workplace*, chapter 9.
16. An extended criticism of this approach is given in Hicks, *Religion and the Workplace*, chapter 8.
17. In the US context, the definitive essay on civil religion is Robert Bellah, "Civil Religion in America," *Daedalus* 96 (1967): 1–21. See also Jean-Jacques Rousseau, *The Social Contract* (New York: St. Martin's Press, 1978).
18. Robert Bellah, "Civil Religion in America."
19. For example, see Robert J. Banks and Kimberly Powell, *Faith in Leadership* (San Francisco, CA: Jossey-Bass, 2000); Ledbetter and Banks, *Reviewing Leadership*, op. cit.
20. See, for example, Carl M. Cannon, "Bush and God: Is Presidential Profession of Faith Still Appropriate or Productive?" *National Journal* 1/3/04, and George C. Edwards III and Philip John Davies, *New Challenges for the American Presidency* (New York: Pearson Longman, 2003), pp. 167–8; Bruce Lincoln, "Bush's God Talk," *The Christian Century*, October 5, 2004: 22–9; Ron Suskind, "Without a Doubt: Faith, Certainty and the Presidency of George W. Bush," *New York Times Magazine*, October 17, 2004: 44–51, 64, 102, 106. For more appreciative accounts, see Stephen Mansfield, *The Faith of George W. Bush*; and David Aikman, *A Man of Faith: The Spiritual Journey of George W. Bush* (Nashville, TN: W Publishing/Thomas Nelson, 2004).
21. George W. Bush, *A Charge to Keep* (William Morrow & Company, 1999). The title phrase is taken from what is reportedly Bush's favorite hymn, written by Charles Wesley.
22. George W. Bush, presidential debate, April 2000.
23. Bellah, "Civil Religion in America."
24. George W. Bush, Inaugural address, January 20, 2001. This and the following citations of Bush's speeches are taken from the official www.whitehouse.gov site and they are widely available in the public record.
25. George W. Bush, State of the Union address, January 29, 2003. See also George W. Bush, State of the Union address, 2004: "The momentum of freedom in our world is unmistakable. And it is not carried forward by our power alone. We can trust in that greater power who guides the unfolding of the year. And in all that is to come, we can know that His purposes are just and true." January 20, 2004.
26. See, for example, Mary E. Hunt, "Faith-Based Inertia in the War Years," *Journal of the American Academy of Religion*, 70/4 (December 2002, 869–74), esp. 872.
27. To be sure, the National Cathedral itself is an interesting and complex institution. The Episcopal building is not funded by public dollars but is used for functions closely allied to the government. However limited, even the post-September 11 memorial event included representatives from multiple religious traditions.

28. George W. Bush, Address in the National Cathedral, September 14, 2001.
29. George W. Bush, Inaugural address, January 20, 2001.
30. President Gerald R. Ford was the first to make an official declaration about Ramadan; President William J. Clinton commonly referred to America's "houses of worship" with reference to "churches, synagogues, and mosques."
31. From his Inaugural address: "And some needs and hurts are so deep they will only respond to a mentor's touch or a pastor's prayer. Church and charity, synagogue and mosque lend our communities their humanity, and they will have an honored place in our plans and in our laws." From his 2004 State of the Union speech: "Yet government has often denied social-service grant and contracts to these groups just because they have a cross or a Star of David or a crescent on the wall."
32. The visit occurred on September 17, 2001. The White House archive, http://www. whitehouse.gov/news/releases/2001/09/20010917-11.html, accessed July 5, 2004.
33. "America Widens 'Crusade' on Terror," BBC News online, September 16, 2001. http://news.bbc.co.uk/1/hi/world/americas/1547561.stm, accessed July 5, 2004.
34. See, for example, Rita Nakashima Brock, "The Fiction of Church and State: A Proposal for Greater Freedom of Religion," *Journal of the American Academy of Religion,* 70/4 (December 2002, 855–61). Discussing Bush's announcement of his "Faith-Based Initiative" in early 2001, Nakashima Brock writes: "The administration's list was limited to the monotheisms most familiar to the dominant secular culture and to Christians. Other American religions, such as Hinduism, Santeria, Lakota traditions, Wicca, Voudou, and Buddhism, were missing. I do not believe these were accidental omissions" (p. 856).
35. Judith Plaskow, "Whose Initiative? Whose Faith?," *Journal of the American Academy of Religion,* 70/4 (December 2002, 863–7); Mary C. Churchill, "In Bad Faith? Possibilities and Perils in the Age of Faith-Based Initiatives," *Journal of the American Academy of Religion,* 70/4 (December 2002, 843–53).
36. Janet R. Jakobsen and Rebecca T. Alpert, "Faith Based on What? A Roundtable Discussion," *Journal of the American Academy of Religion,* 70/4 (December 2002, 821–32); see also Churchill, "In Bad Faith?", and Plaskow, "Whose Initiative? Whose Faith?".
37. Rawls, *Political Liberalism.*
38. John Rawls, "The Idea of Public Reason Revisited," *University of Chicago Law Review* 64 (1997): 765–807.
39. John Paul II, *Evangelium Vitae (The Gospel of Life)* (New York: Pauline Books, 1995).
40. Sheryl Henderson Blunt, "Bush Calls for 'Culture Change': In interview, President says new era of responsibility should replace 'feel-good'," ChristianityToday.com, http://www. christianitytoday.com/ct/2004/121/51.0.html
41. Op. cit.
42. Two of the more vocal opponents of Bush's social policies are the evangelical leader of the Sojourners community, Jim Wallis, and Eugene Rivers, a leader of the Ten Point Coalition in Boston, each of whom originally offered significant support to the president on his faith-based initiative but who have come to see his policies as politically motivated and/or misguided.
43. James MacGregor Burns, *Leadership* (New York: Harper Torchbooks, 1978); Ronald A. Heifetz, *Leadership without Easy Answers* (Cambridge, MA: Belknap Press of Harvard University Press, 1994).
44. This is Ron Suskind's (op. cit.) central criticism of Bush's use of his religion in public life.
45. Thomas Jefferson, *Virginia Statute for Establishing Religious Freedom* (1779); James Madison, *Memorial and Remonstrance against Religious Establishments* (1785); John Courtney Murray, *The Problem of Religious Freedom* (Westminster, MD: Newman Press, 1965); Ronald F. Thiemann, *Religion in Public Life: A Dilemma for Democracy* (Washington, DC: Georgetown University Press, 1996).
46. John Locke, *A Letter Concerning Toleration* (Amherst, NY: Prometheus, 1990 [1689]).
47. Terry Price, *Understanding Ethical Failures in Leadership.*

PART TWO

The minds of leaders:
responsibility, necessary sin,
and fairness

4. Abuse, privilege, and the conditions of responsibility for leaders

Terry L. Price

INTRODUCTION

Leaders can be mistaken in their beliefs about the morality of particular kinds of behavior, for example, about the morality of deception, killing, and even torture. They can also be mistaken with respect to the degree to which these kinds of behavior are morally wrong. This follows from an assumption made by standard moral theories, namely, that moral claims can be true or false. If moral claims can be true or false, then moral beliefs, which represent such claims, can sometimes be mistaken. This is equally true for the moral beliefs of leaders. Part of what distinguishes leaders from others, however, is that leaders often have greater power to act on their mistaken beliefs about morality. As a consequence, the mistakes of leaders more readily result in decisions and actions that have a dramatic impact on the lives and livelihoods of great numbers of people.

When this happens, we are left with an important question over and above issues of moral wrongness: to what extent should leaders be held responsible for their immoral decisions and actions? For purposes of assessing the blameworthiness of these leaders, does it matter that their behavior was based not on desires to do what they took to be morally wrong but, rather, on mistaken beliefs about what was morally right? In large part, a determination of whether morally mistaken leaders are blameworthy for their behavior turns on whether we can hold them responsible for their mistaken beliefs. Ethicists have long recognized that ignorance does not excuse an individual's immoral behavior when the individual is blameworthy for his ignorance. In these cases, the ignorance is "culpable" and responsibility for the ignorance translates into responsibility for the behavior. But what should we say about cases in which leaders are not responsible for their mistaken moral beliefs?

In this chapter, I consider the argument that a leader's upbringing can cause mistaken moral beliefs, thereby making his ignorance non-culpable. On this argument, since the leader is not responsible for his moral ignorance, he should not be held responsible for the immoral behavior that results from it.

To analyze this particular account of leader responsibility, I focus primarily on two kinds of upbringing that might contribute to mistaken moral beliefs. Most obviously, we might think that leaders have an excuse for their behavior when they were subjected to a deprived or abusive upbringing. A less obvious grounding for excuse, but one that I think does more philosophical work in the context of an argument about the responsibility of leaders, is the childhood of privilege. I conclude that the notion of privilege might be extended to show that leadership itself can compete with moral responsibility.

"UNFORTUNATE FORMATIVE CIRCUMSTANCES"

In his famous paper "Freedom and Resentment," philosopher P.F. Strawson claims that having "peculiarly unfortunate . . . formative circumstances" sometimes affects a person's responsibility for his behavior.[1] For Strawson, unfortunate formative circumstances can cause a person to be "psychologically abnormal," "morally underdeveloped," "warped," "deranged," or "neurotic."[2] Gary Watson calls these conditions "exempting," because they "show that the agent, temporarily or permanently, globally or locally, is appropriately exempted from the basic demand" that we make of responsible agents.[3] This is "the demand for the manifestation of a reasonable degree of goodwill or regard, on the part of others, not simply towards oneself, but towards all those on whose behalf moral indignation may be felt."[4] By way of example, Watson's article details the case of Robert Harris. This case serves as a backdrop for my analysis of the responsibility of leaders with deprived or abusive upbringings.

Harris murdered two 16-year-olds, John Mayeski and Michael Baker, after stealing their car. The *Los Angeles Times* reported that

> [a]s the two boys walked away, Harris slowly raised the Luger and shot Mayeski in the back . . . Harris chased Baker down a hill into a little valley and shot him four times. Mayeski was still alive when Harris climbed back up the hill . . . Harris walked over to the boy, knelt down, put the Luger to his head and fired . . . Harris drove [the] car to a friend's house . . . Harris walked into the house, carrying the weapons and the bag [containing] the remainder of the slain youths' lunch . . . Harris took the food out of the bag . . . and began eating a hamburger . . . He smiled and . . . [said] it would be amusing . . . to pose as police officers and inform the parents that their sons were killed.[5]

Harris's behavior, especially the way he acted after the murders, tells us a lot about the kind of person he is. Yet, as disturbing as Harris is to us, earlier chapters in his life make it "[n]o wonder" that he turned out to be this way.[6] Harris was educated in cruelty and indifference at home and, later, in prison: "All of the children had monstrous childhoods. But even in the Harris family, . . . the abuse Robert was subjected to was unusual . . . [At age 14] Harris was sentenced to a federal youth detention center [for car theft]. He was one of the youngest inmates there . . . and . . . was raped several times."[7] This case raises important questions about the general conditions of responsibility. Could Harris's peculiarly unfortunate formative circumstances negate his blame-worthiness for what he did? Could his deprived and abusive upbringing have caused him to be mistaken about the morality of his behavior?

Ethical theorist Susan Wolf fashions a hypothetical example that allows us to ask an analogous question about the responsibility of leaders.

> JoJo is the favorite son of Jo the First, an evil and sadistic dictator of a small, unde-veloped country. Because of his father's special feelings for the boy, JoJo is given a special education and is allowed to accompany his father and observe his daily routine. In light of this treatment, it is not surprising that little JoJo takes his father as a role model and develops values very much like Dad's. As an adult, he does many of the same sorts of things his father did, including sending people to prison or to death or to torture chambers on the basis of whim . . . In light of JoJo's heritage and upbringing – both of which he was powerless to control – it is dubious at best that he should be regarded as responsible for what he does.[8]

Wolf concludes that leaders such as JoJo should not be held responsible for their behavior. Her argument is that JoJo lacks "the ability to know the differ-ence between right and wrong . . . [A] person who, even on reflection, cannot see that having someone tortured because he failed to salute you is wrong plainly lacks the requisite ability."[9] This line of reasoning explains, she thinks, "why victims of deprived childhoods as well as victims of misguided societies may not be responsible for their actions."[10]

Wolf's account of responsibility is strongly resisted by other ethical theor-ists such as Michele Moody-Adams, who reminds us of "the notion – defended at least since Aristotle – that an adult agent's ignorance of what she ought to do is, in general, no excuse for wrongdoing."[11] Moody-Adams takes particular aim at "the empirical credentials of the inability thesis."[12] This is the thesis that some people are unable to know the difference between right and wrong. For one thing, since cultural mechanisms for criticism and dissent are present in all social systems, participants can hardly claim ignorance of the possibility that their practices might be wrong.[13] By drawing attention to the empirical credentials of the inability thesis, Moody-Adams exposes a weak-ness in the supposition that leaders might be completely unaware of the morally problematic nature of behaviors such as torture. Many leaders engage in these behaviors not only in the face of political opposition but also against general moral prohibitions within their society. For example, even in JoJo's society, we might assume that torture is not a commonly acceptable form of behavior. JoJo's willingness to resort to this measure is explained by appeal to personal values passed down from his father, not in terms of more widespread social values. It is he, much more so than his society, who is misguided.

JoJo's case, then, is not perfectly analogous to that of "persons who, though acting badly, act in ways that are strongly encouraged by their societies – the slave owners of the 1850s, the Nazis of the 1930s, and many male chauvinists of our fathers' generation."[14] Despite the fact that JoJo holds mistaken moral beliefs that were transmitted to him directly from his father, not unlike racist or sexist beliefs that are sometimes transmitted from father to son, the idiosyncrasy of JoJo's moral beliefs makes for a relevant distinction between his case and cases in which whole societies or majorities within them are subject to systematic moral error. In this respect, JoJo is much closer to the individuals that Strawson exempts from responsibility because they are "peculiarly unfortunate in [their] formative circumstances."[15] Circumstances of deprivation and abuse put some people outside of the norm. So, saying that a person is unfortunate in his circumstances is a relative claim; it is a claim about his fortune as compared to others within his society.[16] Accordingly, if we conclude that a particular person is not responsible for these reasons, then it is because his upbringing makes him different from other people within his society, not because his upbringing inculcates generally accepted, but mistaken, moral beliefs.

Arguments drawing on formative circumstances thus question the responsibility of leaders such as JoJo because the upbringing of these leaders was radically different from the upbringing of most others within their society. To make this kind of argument, its advocates typically produce evidence that a leader's childhood was not only distinctive but also deprived or, more strongly, abusive. Indeed, there is some evidence to suggest, for example, that the leaders Arnold Ludwig calls "the infamous five" had childhoods that might be characterized in this way.[17]

> Hitler, Mao, Mussolini, Stalin, and Pol Pot . . . were alienated, estranged, or openly hostile toward their fathers. Joseph Stalin's father, who periodically beat him and his mother, was a violent alcoholic and was eventually killed in a brawl when Stalin was eleven years old. Pol Pot's parents sent him to live with an older brother and his wife, who adopted him when he was six, so his relationship with his parents was distant or resentful at best, despite his brother's claim about the lack of open conflicts with them. Adolph Hitler's father, who died when he was eight, drank heavily and was brutally violent toward his family. Mussolini's father drank too much, womanized, and was intermittently employed. Mao Zedong hated his father for beating him and his brothers and for shaming him in front of others, and constantly bucked his authority.[18]

Some immoral leaders, we might be inclined to say, received a "special education" in the exercise of power and domination.[19] But is an education of this kind sufficient to explain the inability of such leaders "to know the difference between right and wrong?"[20] The answer to this question depends on how we understand mistaken beliefs about morality.

TWO VARIETIES OF MISTAKEN MORAL BELIEFS

The first thing to notice about any account of leader responsibility that leans heavily on deprivation or abuse in childhood is that it is not at all clear why such an upbringing would make a person mistaken about the content of morality. By *content mistakes*, I have in mind mistakes that are indexed to questions about what types of behavior are morally right and what types of behavior are morally wrong. First, experiencing a deprived or abusive upbringing might equally be said to make one more aware of the wrongness of this kind of behavior. For example, Bill Clinton's experiences as a child might be seen as the source of his empathy for others. Second, moral education is hardly limited to the relationship between parent and child. This is especially true in a society in which the values of one's parents are different from more general social values. In such a society, even children with deprived or abusive upbringings would be exposed to values that condemn the behavior of their parents. The argument that deprivation and abuse impedes moral knowledge is therefore weaker than the argument that a bad culture can make a person unable to know the difference between right and wrong. Generally, it is more difficult to distinguish morally right from morally wrong behaviors in a society in which people are systematically mistaken about the content of morality.

Not all mistaken moral beliefs are about the content of morality. People can also be mistaken about its scope, and these mistakes come in two varieties: mistakes about who is *bound* by moral requirements and mistakes about who is *protected* by these requirements.[21] With respect to the first kind of error, the person mistakenly believes that he is justified in deviating from a moral requirement because it does not apply to him at all or, at least, in his situation. With respect to the second kind of error, the person mistakenly believes that some individuals do not merit the protection of moral requirements. In some cases, these beliefs about who is protected by morality will be connected to beliefs about who is bound by morality. For example, social contract approaches to morality generally assume that the protection of morality's requirements extend only to those who have the requisite abilities for being bound by them. For thinkers such as Thomas Hobbes, the rationale for extending the protections of morality to an individual in the first place is to create an incentive for that individual to adhere to the requirements of morality, thus bringing benefits or preempting harms to other parties of the contract.[22]

We should question the claim that if an individual merits the protection of morality, then that individual is bound by morality. A moral theory committed to this particular connection between the two considerations of scope risks excluding not only animals but also individuals with mental disabilities, psychiatric illnesses, or more standard cognitive degeneration.[23] However, the converse connection between being bound by the requirements of morality and being protected by these requirements is significantly tighter. That is to say, even if it is false that meriting the protection of morality implies being bound by it, we might nevertheless accept that being bound by morality implies meriting its protection. Perhaps what social contract theorists have right is that it is too much to ask people to be bound by the requirements of morality when they are not protected by these requirements. This necessary condition on being bound by morality, namely, that a person is bound by morality only if he is protected by morality, gives us one way to think about the mistaken moral beliefs of individuals with deprived and abusive backgrounds. When coupled with the mistaken moral belief that a person does not merit the protection of morality, this condition generates the conclusion that he is not bound by its requirements.

To see how individuals with deprived or abusive backgrounds might be especially susceptible to such beliefs, let us return to Watson's analysis of the case of Robert Harris. According to Watson,

> Harris's cruelty is a response to the shattering abuse he suffered during the process of socialization. The objects of his hatred were not just the boys he so exultantly murdered, but the 'moral order' that mauled and rejected him ... He defies the demand for human consideration *because he has been denied this consideration himself.* The mistreatment he received becomes a ground as well as a cause of the mistreatment he gives.[24]

In other words, Harris has come to see himself outside of the moral community. Membership in the moral community minimally entails the protection of moral requirements, and Harris's upbringing has given him good reason to believe that he does not merit this kind of protection. On the assumption that he is not a member of the moral community, it would follow that he is not bound by the requirements of morality. Of course, this assumption is false. Harris is a genuine member of the moral community, fully meriting its protections. But there is reason to think that he does not know this, and we can hardly blame him if it turns out that he is completely ignorant on this point. Nor can we fully blame him for the conclusion that he draws from it, namely, that the requirements of morality do not apply to him.

Perhaps leaders with deprived and abusive backgrounds are similarly mistaken about the scope of morality, not its content. In other words, they recognize that behaviors such as torture are prohibited by morality, but they fail to recognize that these prohibitions apply to them. On this understanding of the immoral behavior of leaders, their ruthlessness and brutality are a reaction to a faulty moral system; one that allowed them to be exposed to ruthlessness and brutality. Since the system did not protect them as children, they will not be bound by it as adults. Yet even this way of understanding why leaders might hold mistaken moral beliefs raises important empirical questions.[25]

These questions are not about the causal connection between deprivation and abuse, on the one hand, and moral ignorance, on the other. As we have seen, by distinguishing between general knowledge about morality's content and more particularized knowledge about its scope, an account of the causes of moral ignorance can make this connection explicit. Rather, the empirical questions raised by this understanding of why some leaders hold mistaken moral beliefs are about the deprivation and abuse, or the extent of deprivation and abuse, experienced by these leaders.

Philosopher David Jones, for example, considers the "possibility that the development of Hitler's character was 'arrested' by harmful experiences or conditions within the family over which he had no control."[26] Jones rejects this possibility, however, on the grounds that "most accounts tend to describe Hitler's father as having been gruff, but more bluster than bite. In addition, there is ample evidence ... that Hitler's mother doted on him and that in general he led a carefree and even pampered existence as a youth."[27] For the purposes of assessing Hitler's blameworthiness, this might just mean that he can be held fully responsible for his behavior. Still, the gravity of the wrong-doing associated with Hitler seems almost to cry out for a deeper explanation, one that appeals to his beliefs about the world and his place in it.[28] As Wolf makes the point, "severely deviant behavior, such as that of a serial murderer or a sadistic dictator, does constitute evidence of a psychological defect in the agent."[29] An alternative to understanding Hitler's moral ignorance as completely culpable, then, would be to locate a "psychological defect" caused by potentially exculpating conditions other than a deprived and abusive childhood. But what else could cause this kind of defect in leaders such as Hitler?

FORTUNATE FORMATIVE CIRCUMSTANCES

A deprived or abusive background is hardly necessary for becoming an adult who engages in ruthless and brutal conduct.[30] As Watson notes,

> someone who had a supportive and loving environment as a child, but who was devoted to dominating others, who killed for enjoyment, would not be vicious in the way Harris is, since he or she could not be seen as striking back at "society"; but such a person could be just *as* vicious. In common parlance, we sometimes call such people "bad apples," a phrase that marks a blank in our understanding. In contrast to Harris, whose malice is motivated, the conduct of "bad apples" seems inexplicable ... However, do we not suppose that *something* must have gone wrong in the developmental histories of these individuals, if not in their socialization, then "in them" – in their genes or brains?[31]

In the absence of evidence of deprivation or abuse, Watson moves rather quickly to more *natural* explanations of the behavior of the so-called bad apples. Here, the suggestion is that the behavior of these individuals can be traced to heredity or to neurological abnormalities. But might there be other appeals to *nurture* that would serve to explain the behavior of some bad apples? In this section, I want to defend the notion that mistaken moral beliefs might also be caused by peculiarly *fortunate* formative circumstances. According to this argument, a privileged upbringing can contribute to a leader's mistaken moral belief that he is outside of the scope of morality.

It is no doubt true that many leaders experienced very difficult childhoods. Ludwig says of the Central African Republic's Eddine Ahmed Bokassa, "it seems reasonable to assume that his traumatic childhood must have warped his psyche. His father, who was the local headsman of his tribe, was jailed and then beaten to death by company officials."[32] Shortly thereafter, Bokassa's mother killed herself. Similarly, Manuel Noriega's mother "died a couple of days after he was born, and his father abandoned him when he was five."[33] Ludwig points out that "Saddam Hussein also had a difficult childhood. His father had died before he was born, and his mother essentially abandoned him to be raised by his uncle."[34] But it is equally true that many future leaders, even particularly immoral ones, were raised in rather supportive environments, not under especially difficult, much less deprived and abusive, conditions. For example, Augusto Pinochet of Chile "was the first of six children and his mother's favorite," and Haiti's Jean-Claude Duvalier, or "Baby Doc," was a "spoiled child" whose mother "came up with the clever idea of special tutoring for Jean-Claude with somebody else taking notes while he slept."[35] Indonesia's Sukarno "spent much time during his childhood with his grand-mother, who believed he was a saint with supernatural powers and made him lick the bodies of sick villagers to cure them of their maladies."[36]

The childhoods of many future leaders are more than supportive. In fact, we might properly describe the childhoods of some future leaders as being privileged. Probably no leader was more privileged as a child than Egypt's King Farouk I, who reigned from 1936 to 1952. According to Ludwig, Farouk

> grew up in palatial splendor, with nursemaids and servants devoted to making all of his infantile wishes come true. As the only son of his parents, King Faud I and Queen Nazri, and with only two half-sisters, he was the natural heir to the throne ... Bored by her life in her husband's harem, [Farouk's mother] turned all her attention on her precious son ... He was pampered, prettified, doted on, fawned on, and indulged by his mother and the other women in the harem ... At the appropriate age, [his] parents secured a private tutor for him, since attending school with children of lesser rank would be unseemly for a future ruler. To prepare him for wisely ruling his kingdom, his tutor taught him about his divine right to rule and his genealogical connections with the Prophet Muhammad ...[37]

It is hard to imagine that this kind of environment would have no effect on Farouk's behavior as a child. As we might expect, "[Farouk was] occasionally given to rages when he didn't get his way. He also liked to throw things. One of his favorite games was to smash rare vases or to grab his pet kitten by the tail and toss it around the room."[38] It is equally hard to imagine that this kind of environment would have no effect on Farouk's behavior as an adult. Again, in keeping with our expectations, "he loved to play practical jokes, the more embarrassing to people the better."[39] After becoming king at the age of 16, Farouk's "gluttony helped him to grow to over 330 pounds. With the reputation of a playboy, he soon became renowned throughout the world for his womanizing, partying, and extravagances."[40] Ultimately, according to the *Encyclopedia of Heads of States and Governments 1900 through 1945*, "His regime was ... viewed as corrupt, and the King's self-indulgent playboy lifestyle did little to endear him to the Egyptian people. [In 1952] Farouk was forced to abdicate in favor of his infant son."[41] Egypt became a republic a year later.

What is the explanation of King Farouk's behavior? One relatively straightforward explanation is that he was reared to see himself as outside of the scope of morality. Throughout his childhood, "[a]s the object of all this attention, he already was preparing for his later role as king."[42] It would be unsurprising, then, if he came to believe that generally accepted moral requirements applied to him neither as a child nor as king in adulthood, even though these requirements applied to others. However, unlike our analysis of Harris, whose deprivation and abuse may have led him to see himself as "being beyond the boundaries of moral community,"[43] it makes more sense to say that leaders such as Farouk see themselves as being *above* the moral community than that they see themselves as being *beneath* it. In other words, the mistaken moral beliefs in question are fundamentally mistakes about who is bound by its moral requirements. These mistaken moral beliefs, that is, are not derived from an assumption on the part of leaders that they are not good enough to be protected by morality. The foundational moral mistake is to think that one is too good, too important, or too special to be bound by these requirements. This is what makes leaders different from others.

Accordingly, if the upbringing of leaders such as Hitler is to support the claim that moral ignorance lessens their responsibility, then the requisite causal story is best served by appealing directly to a particular kind of mistake, a mistake that itself has a particular kind of childhood cause. First, properly identifying the relevant mistake as an error about the scope of morality firms up the causal connection between childhood experiences and moral ignorance. As compared to mistakes about the content of morality, scope mistakes are much easier to explain by appeals to childhood experiences. Second, properly identifying privilege as the particular childhood cause answers empirical questions that arise in those cases in which deprivation and abuse are absent. So, Jones's claim that "there is ample evidence ... that Hitler's mother doted on him and that in general he led a carefree and even pampered existence as a youth"[44] need not detract from efforts to trace "a psychological defect"[45] to his upbringing. In fact, privilege, much more than deprivation and abuse, would seem apt to produce the critical moral mistake Jones assigns to Hitler: "Only I and my interests count in the world; everything else is of secondary importance or of no value."[46] This is not the belief of someone who doubts whether he is good enough to be protected by morality. This is the belief of someone who does not see himself as bound by its requirements.

We can similarly explain the mistaken beliefs of Wolf's hypothetical leader JoJo. As we have seen, there is no need to assume that JoJo's moral ignorance is so extensive that he fails to recognize commonly accepted moral prohibitions against imprisonment, torture, and killing. We need only assume that he is ignorant of the application of these prohibitions to his own behavior. Surely a large part of the explanation for why JoJo might think that he is special enough not to be bound by commonly accepted prohibitions is that he was reared to see himself as being outside of the scope of morality. His mistakes of scope can be traced, that is, not to a deprived or abusive childhood, which might have led him to believe that he did not deserve the protections of moral requirements, but to a privileged childhood, which encouraged him to believe that he deserved exceptions when it came to the application of these requirements. Instead of underestimating his desert as a moral agent, he overestimated it. Here, our causal story need look no further than to JoJo's father's "special feelings" and the "special education" JoJo received as a child.[47] JoJo was taught that ordinary rules apply only to ordinary people. In effect, he was taught that the rules of morality do not apply to dictators.[48]

LEADERSHIP AS A RESPONSIBILITY-UNDERMINING CONDITION

What are the implications of this account of moral ignorance? As part of a larger theory of responsibility, mistakes about the scope of morality would call into question the blameworthiness of leaders from privileged backgrounds when such leaders act on these mistakes. To be plausible, however, a theory of responsibility that accommodates scope mistakes in this fashion must concede that responsibility is on a continuum. Leaders, like all moral agents, can be more or less responsible for their behavior. For example, twenty-first-century men and women who are committed to racist ideologies are clearly more responsible for their mistaken moral beliefs than were eighteenth-century proponents of slavery. This is because moral correction on issues of race is easier for our contemporaries than it was for our ancestors. Similarly, a leader reared in an extremely abusive environment might be less responsible than a leader who was reared under conditions of minimal deprivation, and the privileged upbringing of a future king might be more excusing than the childhood of privilege typical of the English aristocrat.

This is just to say that there will always be empirical questions about how difficult moral correction is for leaders who see themselves as being outside of the scope of morality. Only when the answers to these empirical questions make it unreasonable to suggest that a leader should have corrected his beliefs can we say that he is not responsible for his behavior. In the cases at hand, assessments of the difficulty of moral correction will turn on the effects of the abuse and deprivation or, alternatively, on the effects of the privilege. For some leaders, these empirical questions will hardly be easy to answer. With respect to questions about deprivation and abuse, we do know that leaders such as Clinton were reared under relatively difficult conditions. Clinton's father died before he was born, and Clinton's stepfather was a violent alcoholic.[49] Likewise, we are in a good position to characterize the upbringing of leaders reared within politically powerful families such as the Kennedys and the Bushes as childhoods of privilege.[50] These early influences may well play an important role in an explanation of private exception making on the part of Clinton and some members of the Kennedy family as well as the pubic exception making on the part of George W. Bush.[51] That said, it would be hard to establish with any degree of certainty the extent to which these childhood experiences impeded leaders' capacity for moral correction.

A more important empirical consideration for an account of leader responsibility is that many leaders, even those notorious for their ethical failings, had surprisingly conventional upbringings. This is especially true for leaders in democratic societies.[52] With respect to most democratic leaders, that is, we can be fairly confident that their childhoods were neither particularly abusive and deprived nor particularly privileged. Richard Nixon, for example, "was raised in a relatively joyless lower-middle-class household located in the small town of Whittier, California."[53] Indeed, according to Ludwig, "Nixon typifies the kind of childhood . . . commonly found in leaders of established democracies . . . Like Nixon, the greatest proportion of democratic rulers came from middle-class backgrounds."[54] It is worth noting that research does suggest that future leaders are generally more privileged than their followers. On Bernard Bass's analysis, "taken as a whole, the evidence presented in studies from a wide variety of leadership situations indicated that leaders tend to come from a socioeconomic background that is superior to that of the average of their followers."[55] In other words, even if future leaders are not typically reared under conditions of absolute privilege, it is nevertheless likely that they will be relatively privileged in leadership contexts. Still, we would be hard pressed to appeal to a relatively good upbringing to explain, let alone excuse, Nixon's behavior or the immoral behavior of most other democratic leaders.

A second respect in which leaders differ from followers better lends itself to a general argument from privilege. From the fact that a leader was reared in conventional family settings, it does not follow that his childhood itself was conventional. This is because the influences of childhood extend well beyond parenting and the household. As Ludwig's research makes clear, most future leaders are set apart by their leadership experiences as children and young adults.[56]

> The inclination of these children and youths to show leadership abilities even shows up in how they play games . . . As a teenager, [Indira Gandhi] organized her own party, called the monkey brigade, and recruited many children to it. She drilled them, marched them, and issued orders to them about their duties . . . As a child, Charles de Gaulle . . . often played tin soldiers with his brothers and other relatives [to whom Charles made political and military assignments] . . . Charles always would be the king of France and commander of the French army. Whenever anyone else wanted to trade positions with him, Charles would indignantly protest, 'Never! France is mine!'[57]

Like Indira Gandhi and Charles de Gaulle, Yassir Arafat, "[b]y the time he was ten years old, . . . was training and drilling all the children in the neighborhood to become Arab guerrilla fighters, and, by the time he was in college, he assumed authority over all aspects of Palestinian students' lives."[58] The tendencies exemplified by these future leaders are indicative of a behavioral characteristic Ludwig refers to as "[b]ureaucratizing the group."[59] Future leaders also exhibit what Ludwig calls "contrariness": they rebel against parents, challenge school authorities, defy traditional religious beliefs, challenge the authority of the party, and disregard social customs.[60] Fidel Castro, for example, "organized a group of workers against his father, who owned a sugar plantation, because he felt his father was exploiting them," and "Mao was one of the first students to cut off his pigtail to signify his independence."[61]

Perhaps these childhood experiences have the most important effect on the way leaders think about themselves and their place in the moral community. After all, commonly accepted moral requirements are regularly aligned with parental values, education, religion, and social custom. Of course, leaders such as Castro may sincerely believe – both in their youth and as adults – that they are justified in violating these requirements. But this is just the point. Given particular leadership experiences as children and, more specifically, the success of these experiences, leaders can grow up to believe that they are somehow beyond the scope of morality. As a teenager, for example, Mao "began shocking his schoolmates by wearing eccentric, outlandish outfits; interrupting boring teachers with nasty remarks; revolting against all forms of discipline; and reveling in his rebelliousness. As a consequence of these and other activities, his fellow students voted him 'student of the year' and elected him secretary to the Student Society."[62] The early leadership behavior exhibited by future leaders such as Castro and Mao thus contrasts sharply with *rule follow-ing*. In fact, it is better described as *rule breaking* or, as in the childhoods of Indira Gandhi, de Gaulle, and Arafat, as *rule making*.[63] This is just what we should expect given what it means to *rule*: "to control, guide, direct, exercise sway or influence."[64] It is the *ruled*, not the *rulers*, who are "subjected to control, guidance, or discipline."[65]

For purposes of assessing responsibility, does it matter that these future leaders *choose* to engage in activities that potentially give rise to mistakes about the scope of morality? In other words, what is the relevance of the fact that childhood leadership experiences, unlike family circumstances and upbringing, are within the control of future leaders? Here, we might think specifically about future leaders who "set out deliberately to transform their nature into one that is more suitable for rulers."[66] By way of example, Theodore Roosevelt "set out to change his nature," and "[w]hen [Winston Churchill] was seven, he deliberately decided to be different . . . to become a great orator and a hero."[67] More appropriate for a discussion of leader immorality is the case of Nixon, who "assumed a leadership role in the many organizations he joined because of deliberate decisions on his part."[68] Clearly, for thinkers in the Aristotelian tradition, the presence of this kind of voluntary choice is sufficient for holding leaders responsible for their ignorance as well as for any immoral behavior that might follow from it. Our characters make us "inattentive," and we are ultimately responsible for our characters, since "[o]nly a totally insensible person would not know that each type of activity is the source of the corresponding state; hence if someone does what he knows will make him unjust, he is willingly unjust."[69]

This Aristotelian line objection to using ignorance as an excuse assumes that people should know the consequences of their actions on their moral beliefs. Maybe this assumption is a plausible one to make with respect to the activities Aristotle has in mind: "living carelessly," "being unjust by cheating," and "being intemperate by passing [the] time in drinking and the like."[70] But the assumption is much less plausible with respect to the activity of leadership. Why should we expect future leaders or, for that matter, current leaders to know that their choices to exercise leadership risk causing them to hold mistaken beliefs about the scope of morality? If we cannot reasonably make this expectation of leaders, and I think that we cannot, then we must be open to the possibility that leadership itself can compete with responsibility. On this possibility, the capacity of leaders to act as morally responsible agents is threatened by the inherent privileges of leadership, no less than by a deprived, abusive, or privileged upbringing. Holding leaders responsible for their behav-ior therefore demands that we make leaders aware – both in leadership train-ing and in their public lives as leaders – of the risk of coming to accept mistaken beliefs about the scope of morality.

NOTES

1. Peter Strawson, "Freedom and Resentment," in John Martin Fischer and Mark Ravizza (eds), *Perspectives on Moral Responsibility* (Ithaca, NY: Cornell University Press, 1993), p. 52.
2. Strawson, "Freedom and Resentment," p. 52.
3. Gary Watson, "Responsibility and the Limits of Evil: Variations on a Strawsonian Theme," in Ferdinand Schoeman (ed.), *Responsibility, Character, and the Emotions: New Essays in Moral Psychology* (Cambridge: Cambridge University Press, 1987), p. 260.
4. Strawson, "Freedom and Resentment," p. 57.
5. Quoted in Watson, "Responsibility and the Limits of Evil," p. 269.
6. Watson, "Responsibility and the Limits of Evil," p. 275.
7. Quoted in Watson, "Responsibility and the Limits of Evil," pp. 272–3.
8. Susan Wolf, "Sanity and the Metaphysics of Responsibility," in Ferdinand Schoeman (ed.), *Responsibility, Character, and the Emotions: New Essays in Moral Psychology* (Cambridge: Cambridge University Press, 1987), pp. 53–4.
9. Wolf, "Sanity and the Metaphysics of Responsibility," p. 56.
10. Wolf, "Sanity and the Metaphysics of Responsibility," p. 57.
11. Michele M. Moody-Adams, "Culture, Responsibility, and Affected Ignorance," *Ethics*, 104 (1994): 293.
12. Moody-Adams, "Culture, Responsibility, and Affected Ignorance," p. 294.
13. I argue in *Understanding Ethical Failures in Leadership* (New York: Cambridge University Press, 2006), chapter 7, that recognizing the possibility that one's practices might be wrong only gets one so far in a moral analysis of those practices.
14. Wolf, "Sanity and the Metaphysics of Responsibility," pp. 56–7.
15. Strawson, "Freedom and Resentment," p. 52.
16. I do not mean to imply by my use of "fortune" that these circumstances are outside of human control.
17. Arnold M. Ludwig, *King of the Mountain: The Nature of Political Leadership* (Lexington, KY: University Press of Kentucky, 2002), p. 152.
18. Ludwig, *King of the Mountain*, p. 152.
19. Wolf, "Sanity and the Metaphysics of Responsibility," p. 53.
20. Wolf, "Sanity and the Metaphysics of Responsibility," p. 56.
21. See, for example, Terry L. Price, "Explaining Ethical Failures of Leadership," *Leadership and Organization Development Journal*, 21 (2000): 177–84. Reprinted with revisions in Joanne B. Ciulla (ed.), *Ethics, the Heart of Leadership*, 2nd edn (Westport, CT: Praeger, 2004), pp. 129–46. These distinctions serve as the basis for the main argument in my *Understanding Ethical Failures in Leadership: The Moral Psychology of Exception Making*.
22. Allen Buchanan, "Justice as Reciprocity versus Subject-Centered Justice," *Philosophy and Public Affairs*, 19 (1990): 227–52.
23. See, for example, Peter Carruthers, *The Animals Issue: Moral Theory in Practice* (Cambridge: Cambridge University Press, 1992).
24. Watson, "Responsibility and the Limits of Evil," p. 277 (emphasis added).
25. It also fails to show what makes leaders different from others.
26. David H. Jones, *Moral Responsibility in the Holocaust: A Study in the Ethics of Character* (Lanham, MD: Rowman and Littlefield, 1999), pp. 137–8.
27. Jones, *Moral Responsibility in the Holocaust*, p. 138.
28. On the issue of moral ignorance, biographer Hugh Trevor-Roper claims that "Hitler was convinced of his own rectitude." Quoted in Ron Rosenbaum, *Explaining Hitler: The Search for the Origins of His Evil* (New York: Random House, 1998), p. 69.
29. Wolf, "Sanity and the Metaphysics of Responsibility," p. 61.
30. Nor is it sufficient. See, for example, Watson's claim that "the force of the [Harris] example does not depend on a belief in the *inevitability* of the upshot" ("Responsibility and the Limits of Evil," p. 275).
31. Watson, "Responsibility and the Limits of Evil," pp. 277–8.

32. Ludwig, *King of the Mountain*, p. 143.
33. Ludwig, *King of the Mountain*, p. 143.
34. Ludwig, *King of the Mountain*, p. 144.
35. Ludwig, *King of the Mountain*, pp. 138, 147.
36. Ludwig, *King of the Mountain*, p. 150.
37. Ludwig, *King of the Mountain*, pp. 129–31.
38. Ludwig, *King of the Mountain*, p. 130. One of Saddam Hussein's "favorite amusements was to heat the bar he carried for protection over a fire and then stab an animal in the stomach as it passed by. With practice he became so good at this that he could rip the animal open and almost split it in half with one stroke" (Ludwig, *King of the Mountain*, p. 145).
39. Ludwig, *King of the Mountain*, p. 130.
40. Ludwig, *King of the Mountain*, pp. 136–7.
41. Harris M. Lentz III, *Encyclopedia of Heads of States and Governments 1900 through 1945* (Jefferson, NC: McFarland and Company, 1999), pp. 139–40.
42. Ludwig, *King of the Mountain*, p. 130.
43. Watson, "Responsibility and the Limits of Evil," p. 271.
44. Jones, *Moral Responsibility in the Holocaust*, p. 138.
45. Wolf, "Sanity and the Metaphysics of Responsibility," p. 61.
46. Jones, *Moral Responsibility in the Holocaust*, p. 139.
47. Wolf, "Sanity and the Metaphysics of Responsibility," p. 53.
48. The first version of Immanuel Kant's categorical imperative, as well as the golden rule, seems designed to prevent such mistakes.
49. See, for example, Eleanor Clift and Jonathan Atler, "You Didn't Reveal Your Pain," *Newsweek* (March 30, 1992): 37; and Garry Wills, "Clinton's Forgotten Childhood," *Time* (June 8, 1992): 62.
50. At the 1988 Democratic National Convention, Ann Richards, state treasurer and later governor of Texas, famously said of George H.W. Bush: "Poor George, he can't help it – he was born with a silver foot in his mouth" ("Transcript of the Keynote Address by Ann Richards, the Texas Treasurer," *New York Times*, July 19, 1988).
51. Here, I have in mind Bush administration statements on the applicability of the Geneva Conventions to prisoners of war in Afghanistan and Iraq as well as its efforts to keep American soldiers outside the jurisdiction of the International Criminal Court.
52. Ludwig, *King of the Mountain*, p. 165.
53. Ludwig, *King of the Mountain*, p. 163.
54. Ludwig, *King of the Mountain*, p. 165.
55. Bernard M. Bass, *Bass and Stogdill's Handbook of Leadership: Theory, Research, and Managerial Applications*, 3rd edn (New York: Free Press, 1990), p. 71.
56. For a litany of examples, see Ludwig, *King of the Mountain*, p. 166.
57. Ludwig, *King of the Mountain*, pp. 166–7.
58. Ludwig, *King of the Mountain*, p. 328.
59. Ludwig, *King of the Mountain*, p. 327.
60. Ludwig, *King of the Mountain*, pp. 330–33.
61. Ludwig, *King of the Mountain*, pp. 331, 329.
62. Ludwig, *King of the Mountain*, p. 329.
63. See, for example, E.P. Hollander, *Leaders, Groups, and Influence* (New York: Oxford University Press, 1964).
64. "Rule," def. 1a, *The Oxford English Dictionary*, 2nd edn, vol. 14 (Oxford: Clarendon Press, 1989), p. 230.
65. "Ruled," def. 1a, *The Oxford English Dictionary*, 2nd edn, vol. 14 (Oxford: Clarendon Press, 1989), p. 232.
66. Ludwig, *King of the Mountain*, p. 167.
67. Ludwig, *King of the Mountain*, p. 167.
68. Ludwig, *King of the Mountain*, p. 165.
69. Aristotle, *Nicomachean Ethics*, trans. Terence Irwin (Indianapolis: Hackett, 1985), pp. 67–8 [1114a3–13].
70. Aristotle, *Nicomachean Ethics*, p. 67 [1114a4–6].

5. "Oh Lord, Won't You Buy Me a Mercedes-Benz": how compensation practices are undermining the credibility of executive leaders

Jay A. Conger

The singer Janis Joplin penned a song entitled "Oh Lord, Won't You Buy Me a Mercedes Benz" in which she playfully implores God to provide her with a number of the extravagant niceties in life. There is a striking parallel between the attitude and desire conveyed in this song and those of executives of America's publicly traded corporations when it comes to their own compensation. For more than a decade, the news headlines have highlighted the fact that executives have been largely successful in getting most of what they want: "Crony Capitalism," "A Decade of Executive Excess: The 1990s," and "CEO Compensation: Time for Reform." These headlines and their stories chronicle a trend in the business world to reward senior business leaders with excessive levels of compensation. For example, the median CEO compensation of a majority sample of Fortune 500 companies in 2003 was $7.1 million. Those in the Fortune 100 averaged $12.2 million. In 2002, the average US CEO earned 282 times what the average employee did. This compares to a ratio of 42 to one in 1980.[1] But these are average figures. At the extreme end of the spectrum, there is Larry Gulp, CEO of Danaher, who received $53 million in 2003 compensation or Steve Jobs, CEO of Apple Computer, who took home $74.8 million.[2] In essence, compensation at the top continues to be excessive and has even become corrupt in some firms. As a byproduct, it is not uncommon to find executives possessing an entitlement mentality that far exceeds the bounds of reasonable rewards for performance. These excessive payouts do more harm than good – undermining the credibility of executive leaders and reinforcing incentives for many executives to manage the financial performance of their firms for the short term rather than for long-term growth and value.

The two-decade bull market of the 1980s and 1990s fueled the recent compensation boom and brought media attention to executives at well known companies like Enron, WorldCom, and Disney for their exorbitant pay packages. The "poster boy," however, of this era was one Dennis Kozlowski, former chairman and CEO of Tyco International, an industrial conglomerate. Under Mr Kozlowski's leadership, a former government laboratory with $3 billion in revenues was transformed into a $36 billion conglomerate and Wall Street darling. His compensation mirrored the spectacular growth in his firm. In 1992, his salary stood at $950,000. By 1997, total compensation had jumped to $26 million. Then one year later it reached $70 million. By 2000, his compensation package was some $137 million. Indicted for evading state taxes on personal purchases of multi-million dollar artwork, he would later be charged under a second indictment with defrauding Tyco of more than $300 million. According to court filings in 1998, he charged Tyco International for $52,334 in wine, $96,943 in flowers, $155,067 in clothing, and $72,042 in jewelry. He hosted a $2.1 million birthday party for his wife of which some $1 million was paid by Tyco according to court records. In 2000, without consulting his board, he decided to "forgive" a large portion of a personal relocation loan which included $19.4 million for the purchase of his home and land in Florida.[3] Kozlowski's sense of entitlement had no apparent bounds.

The critical question of course is whether executives like Kozlowski represent a small handful of individuals or the tip of a far larger iceberg encompassing the corporate world. In other words, was he one of a few bad apples among corporate chieftains or is the apple barrel itself rotten? As Kim Clark, dean of the Harvard Business School, argues, how one answers this question profoundly determines what can and should be done to address executive compensation abuses. For example, if the conclusion is that a small number of executives are at fault, then the solution is fairly straightforward: prosecute the "bad apples," fine and jail them, and hope that punishment and publicity will curb the inclinations of the remaining bad ones. If the barrel is the real problem, then the solutions must be far more systematic and widespread. They must involve revamping corporate governance and boardroom oversight as well as instituting new regulations and tax codes.[4] My experience in boardrooms and in the world of business tells me that the barrel itself has a serious degree of rot. In this chapter, I will discuss the forces that have been undermining the integrity of that barrel and offer suggestions as to how we might mend executive compensation and restore credibility to executive leadership in the process.

As a caveat, this is a very difficult barrel to mend. The problem is a recurrent one. Numerous attempts to remedy it have had very limited success. To illustrate its long history, we can look back to 1929 when Eugene Grace, CEO of Bethlehem Steel, received an annual salary of $12,000 which in those times was considered a great deal of money. That same year, because of the performance of the company, he was awarded a bonus of $1.2 million – a truly remarkable and groundbreaking sum for a professional manager. As a result, he became the first millionaire of a publicly traded company in American history.[5] Before that time, business people who became millionaires were entrepreneurs, the builders of companies; individuals such as DuPont, Vanderbilt, Rockefeller rather than professional managers. By the first half of the twentieth century, however, entrepreneurial builders were no longer leading many of the nation's largest companies – the very firms they had built. Rather the leadership of these firms was in the hands of professional managers. The exuberant stock market of the 1920s had encouraged rewards based on stock performance (a striking parallel to the 1990s), and Grace at Bethlehem Steel became one of the most prominent beneficiaries. That said, it was not until 1933 (in the midst of the Great Depression) that the issue of executive compensation created a genuine firestorm. In that year, George Washington Hill, who was the head of American Tobacco, received a bonus of $1.3 million. The shareholders took him to court over what they perceived as excessive pay. It was the first lawsuit over CEO pay. The Supreme Court decided that pay could be subject to judicial review at public companies.[6] This set in motion the first regulations concerning CEO compensation. As an outcome, CEO pay had to be approved at the company's shareholders' meetings. As we have witnessed over the last decade, this safeguard, however, proved to have limited efficacy.

HOW AND WHY THE EXECUTIVE COMPENSATION BARREL DEVELOPED A PERENNIAL PROBLEM WITH ROT

The executive compensation barrel is a complex one made of many planks which are subject to an array of forces. One of the most powerful forces that historically causes "barrel rot" is a booming equity market. For example, the equity markets of the roaring 20s and 90s both induced excessive levels of executive compensation. A more durable and fundamental contributor is the capitalist orientation of the United States. America is at its heart a society built around the notion of individual achievement and reward with a strong emphasis on acquiring personal wealth as a measure of one's success. This is apparent even among the youngest members of society. In the annual survey of freshman college students conducted by UCLA, one question asked of the incoming freshman across the country is "what are your priorities as a young person?" In 2003, 74 percent of all freshmen responded "to be financially successful." The only survey item which was ranked more highly is "to raise a family."[7]

But there are other equally weighty contributors which make it difficult for the barrel's integrity to withstand the pressure of the first two forces. The most influential of these include: (1) the nature of corporate boards and their relationship with the CEO, (2) fundamental shifts in compensation practices over the last two decades, (3) our tendency to romance the influence of the CEO role, (4) executive narcissism and an accompanying sense of entitlement and (5) public conceptions of the purpose of corporations. We will start with the first of these – the corporate boardroom – where safeguards should have been in place.

Boardroom Leadership

In most US corporations, the chief executive officer is the de facto leader of the boardroom. The CEO's authority is further reinforced by the fact that most CEOs also hold the position of board chairman. In other words, formal leadership rests entirely in their hands. This is due in large part to the natural advantages of their position. As CEO, they have far greater access to current and comprehensive information about the state of the company than other board members. In contrast, the typical director's knowledge about company affairs is extremely limited given their part-time role and their status as outsiders. Most directors are all too aware of this gap in their own understanding and therefore often concede authority to the CEO. In addition, most directors see their first role as serving the CEO and their secondary role as providing oversight. This belief is fostered by the fact that most board directors of publicly traded companies are CEOs themselves, and they share in an etiquette that suggests restraint from aggressively challenging or from meddling too deeply into the details of a fellow CEO's business. These dynamics encourage directors under most circumstances to defer to the CEO's judgment. As a result, the CEO normally determines the agenda for meetings and controls much of the information that directors receive.[8] The CEO often selects who sits on the board and who is a member of the board's committees. While new government regulations and governance practices are being introduced to counter such outcomes, only in the last few years are they having an impact. Outside of a serious decline in company performance or a scandal, CEOs continue to "lead" most boardrooms.

In the case of executive compensation, the dilemma with the "CEO model" of board leadership is that it lacks an effective system of checks and balances. If a CEO feels quite strongly that he and his executive team deserve a certain pay package, his strong leadership position ensures a high probability of receiving that package. Given that most board members today are CEOs, the board is further prejudiced towards the award of generous pay packages based often on an implicit notion of reciprocity: the "I'll-scratch-your-back-if-you'll-scratch-mine" principle.[9] Moreover, a study by Governance Metric

International reveals that one out of every twelve public traded corporations has a CEO who sits on the board of another company led by a member of his own board of directors.[10] Since the stakes are high given the large sums of money involved in executive compensation and directors' personal ties to the CEO, executive compensation decisions can encourage collusive behavior in the boardroom. Directors may have an explicit or implicit agreement to give the executive team positive evaluations and in return high levels of compensation. Even in situations where directors take the task of evaluating the compensation of the executive team in a rigorous and objective manner, there is another factor that leads them to make favorable compensation decisions. Their compensation assessments depend heavily upon the outside world – in other words, boardroom compensation committees have largely outsourced decision-making.

The Outsourcing of Compensation

Today, compensation decisions for corporate executives are made by the board of directors and the board's compensation committee. That said, the actual evaluation of CEO performance and compensation decisions have been largely outsourced to the market and to consultants. During the bull market of the 1990s, boards and CEOs came to believe that particularly CEO performance should be evaluated by a shareholder value model. In other words, the growth rate of the company's market capitalization or its share price appreciation represented the best measure of company performance and in turn a reflection on the capabilities of a firm's executives. As a result, compensation packages began to include larger and larger stock benefits. In the early 1990s, for example, only approximately 8 percent of a Fortune 500 CEO pay package was in equities. By the end of the 1990s, this percentage hit 66 percent, in other words two-thirds on average of the pay of a CEO of a large publicly traded company was in some form of stock compensation.[11]

In addition, board compensation committees increasingly turned to outsiders for compensation guidance – individuals called compensation consultants. The rationale was a simple one. They could provide benchmark compensation data for executives in comparable companies. The problem was that the consultants came from firms that provided other services beyond compensation advice to their client companies. Their firms also provided executive recruiting, auditing, pension advice, and consulting services. The potential for serious conflict of interest problems arose. For example, executive recruiting firms have a key relationship with the CEO of many firms. How could they declare that their client, the CEO, needed to take a far more modest pay increase without jeopardizing their mainstream recruiting business? A similar predicament is faced by accounting and human resources consulting firms who provide compensation advice. Millions of dollars in lucrative contract work in auditing and consulting are also provided to the same client. A less than attractive compensation proposal for the company's top decision-makers might make the auditing and consulting practices of competitors look far more attractive. As a result, compensation consultants face the age old predicament "Why bite the hand that feeds you." This dependence presumably encourages a built-in bias towards proposing attractive compensation packages for the top decision-makers. As Kim Clark has argued, the use of external consultants in essence has created the Lake Wobegon effect – "in Lake Wobegon, everyone is above average."[12]

In addition, the compensation consultants and the boardroom compensation committees most commonly employ the use of peer groups and competitive benchmarking to determine what is a "fair market" executive compensation package. In 1992, the SEC instituted a new requirement in which publicly-held companies had to report how much their CEOs were paid. While the intention was to create greater transparency around executive pay, this requirement also created a transparent peer group for the benchmarking of compensation.[13] In this case, the peer group employed by the compensation consultants was executives in companies within the same industry and of a similar size. What most boards attempt to do is to keep executive compensation at par or above the median level of the industry peer group. This benchmarking, however, is further contributing to compensation excesses. For example, research discovered that CEOs who are paid below the median level in total compensation of their peer group received pay increases that are twice as large relative to the raises received by CEOs who are paid above the median of their peers.[14] These raises were not only greater in percentage terms but also in absolute dollars. The researchers further discovered that large compensation increases for executives paid below the median of their peer group occurred even when their companies had, on average, worse accounting and stock price performance than their peers.

Romanticizing of the CEO Role

Organizational members, the public, and the media are subject to a psychological phenomenon which is known as "The Romance of Leadership." This well documented phenomenon reveals that human beings desire to attribute much of the control of an organization to a single individual – that being the senior-most leader. Whether or not this individual is actually in control is irrelevant. We simply want to believe they are. The popular hero myths of society further reinforce this stereotype with their emphasis on a single actor who triumphs over daunting challenges.

As Jim Meindl and his colleagues have pointed out, this "romancing" phenomenon is the product of the fact that most organizational events involve multiple determinants and therefore are too complex and difficult to fully comprehend.[15] Members of an organization and interested outsiders, however, want to make sense of this complexity. Because senior leaders are the most visible and have a formal position of authority, there is a strong tendency to attribute the cause of organizational outcomes directly to their actions. In other leadership research, Gary Yukl points out that this process of attribution also reflects societal biases towards explaining outcomes in terms of the rational actions of human beings in contrast to random events or larger forces.[16] Underpinning this belief is the assumption that organizations are themselves largely rational, goal-oriented systems that are seeking to meet the needs of their members and society. Individuals in senior leadership positions come to symbolize the controlling or guiding forces behind this promise of the organization. This in turn encourages organizational members to overemphasize the personal characteristics of their leader and to minimize the situational factors when searching for explanations of outcomes.[17]

This phenomenon of "romancing" is particularly apparent in the press, in business books, and in the financial community where there is a singular focus on the statements and actions of CEOs to explain the successful performance of companies. The dynamic of romancing CEO leadership became particularly pronounced in the 1990s when a large number of "celebrity CEOs" appeared – from Jeff Bezos of Amazon to John Chambers of Cisco to Herb Kelleher of Southwest Airlines to Jack Welch of General Electric. While this attribution does not capture the reality that hundreds or thousands of individuals are actually managing and leading complex organizations, it serves to skew executive compensation decisions. After all, if the organization, the financial community, and the media deeply hold an assumption that a single individual in the CEO role can profoundly influence the performance of an organization, there should be no hesitation in ensuring that person is handsomely compensated. It is imperative to keep them highly motivated and to ensure they remain with the firm rather than depart to a competitor.

Executive Narcissism and Entitlement

At the top of corporations, it is not uncommon to find individuals who are highly narcissistic. Michael Maccoby even argues that there has been a pronounced change in the personality of today's senior business leaders towards greater narcissism.[18] Executives tend to be strongly ambitious and achievement-oriented individuals – qualities lending themselves to a strongly narcissistic personality. This generation of executives is accustomed to a great deal of attention from the media and Wall Street feeding into a sense of self-importance. Narcissists in general fall prey to the romancing of leadership assuming that they are indeed "leading" the enterprise and that much of the firm's success can be directly attributed to their actions. Highly narcissistic individuals also tend to have an intense competitive drive constantly benchmarking everything and everyone.[19] These qualities reveal themselves in executive compensation. For example, it is not uncommon to hear executives rationalize their pay packages by comparing them to those of sports figures or entertainment celebrities who receive multi-million dollar pay contracts. They argue that their own contributions as business leaders overseeing organizations that are providing essential goods and services for the public are far more important than those of the celebrities. Therefore they deserve comparable if not higher rewards. As highly competitive individuals, executives often rationalize their pay and perks using the "equity theory" of compensation, which is most evident in the benchmarking of peer groups. So, for example, they might argue "Eugene Grace of Bethlehem Steel received a $1.2 million stock payout this year. My company is just as big, and so I deserve $1.2 million. Actually I think I'm better than he is, I probably deserve $1.5 million." For instance, I am aware of other executives who rationalize their perks as imperatives to the successful performance of their job. One CEO argued that she required a personal chef as an essential perk. She explained that she did not have time to go down to the cafeteria on the first floor of the building given the demands on her time. Her use of a personal chef would ensure that her day was spent more efficiently. Moreover, as the CEO, she was so valuable that any chance of food poisoning needed to be minimized. By having a chef she could control the quality of her food as well as control her diet and therefore her health.

Dennis Kozlowski, the former CEO of Tyco, was asked why he considered certain personal expenses as ones that he could deduct from the company. He had a very simple rationalization – "We were all about growth. It took thirty-seven million dollars in expenses to affect our earnings even by one percent." James Steward commented "This [rationalization] became a recurring theme: no matter how expensive (his expenditures on company perks) in absolute terms, the costs were insignificant as a percentage of Tyco's revenues and profits."[20]

Notions of the Public Corporation

Throughout the twentieth century, there have been two distinct but conflicting conceptualizations of the public corporation. One is the *property conception*; the other is the *social entity conception*.[21] Under the property conception, the corporation is the private property of the owners or shareholders. Corporate directors are agents of the owners, and it is their role to dutifully advance the financial aims of the "owners." The corporation's purpose is to enrich shareholders. In sharp contrast, the conception of the corporation as a social entity treats the organization as an institution with multiple constituencies. The corporation is no longer simply a private entity responsible solely to its owners but rather it is accountable to the public. It not only serves its community but also has an obligation to act as a model corporate citizen.

Throughout the nineteenth as well as the early and late twentieth century, the property conception has been the dominant conception of the corporation. A pivotal law case, the 1919 Michigan Supreme Court, *Dodge v. Ford Motor Co.* case, epitomized this viewpoint.[22] In their capacity as shareholders, the Dodge brothers had sued the Ford Motor Company arguing that the corporation did not have shareholder welfare as its principal concern. The impetus for the suit was a decision by Henry Ford to suspend indefinitely dividend payments and instead to reinvest some $58 million in company profits so that the company could lower the price of products and to expand the company's business. While Mr Ford had argued that the purpose of a corporation was to produce good products inexpensively, to provide employment, and only "incidentally to make money," the Dodge brothers contested this viewpoint arguing that the shareholders were the owners of the enterprise and that they were entitled to a portion of the accumulated profits. The Michigan Supreme Court sided with the Dodge brothers and ordered Ford to restore the dividends. Underlying its decision, the court highlighted a principal assumption: "A business corporation is organized and carried on primarily for the profit of the stockholders. The powers of the directors are to be employed for that end."[23]

The social entity conception of the corporation first appears in the late nineteenth century with the emergence of the modern business enterprise. At that time, the "owners" of the modern corporation were increasingly outside investors (rather than the entrepreneurial founders) who could and did, easily and at little cost, move funds from company to company.[24] In addition, they were fragmented, which simply reinforced the fact that it was easier to sell than to intervene when top management was ineffective. As control of the corporation shifted towards professional managers, the expertise and freedom of this group to act were soon seen as critical ingredients in shaping the success of the modern day business enterprise. It was felt that the investment maximizing aims of shareholders should take a back seat to the seemingly longer term, value creation aims of professional management. While the contributors of capital were due an attractive rate of return on their investment, there were other constituents to serve – customers, employees, and the community. No longer were directors solely beholden to shareholders but rather they had to balance with management the frequently conflicting claims of the corporation's many constituencies. In turn, the board of directors' duties went beyond "assuring investors a fair return, to include a duty of loyalty in some sense to all those interested in or affected by the corporation."[25]

One can imagine that under the social entity conception, executive compensation would be strongly moderated by a need to distribute company wealth more widely to the employees and the community and to reinvest in the firm. It would be difficult to imagine a CEO paying him or herself excessive amounts of pay since the primary metric or rationale for pay does not rest upon shareholder value. Hoarding large sums of money for oneself would not comfortably align with an organization whose mission is a larger social purpose.

While the property and social entity notions of the corporation have co-existed without a great deal of debate for most of the twentieth century, the takeover movement of the 1980s pushed board directors towards the property conception.[26] For example, when most if not all of the shareholders wished to sell control of the company, whose interests were the directors to promote and protect – shareholders or management? How could a board member turn down a hostile cash tender offer when investors saw it as a wise return on their investment? After all, how could directors turn down a significant financial gain for investors using arguments that future returns might be better?[27] Directors soon found themselves in conflict over their allegiances. The takeover environment had created a situation where it was extremely difficult for directors to convince shareholders that realizing an immediate, substantial profit on their investment was a bad idea. The property conception regained the upper hand. Shareholder value became the central mantra in many boardrooms.

In the 1990s, however, the tug-of-war was intensified when there was a sharp divergence between the decisions of the court and shifts in the market place. Setting the precedent, the Delaware Supreme Court in the *Time Warner* case decided that corporate directors could indeed take actions that prevented shareholders from realizing an immediate high premium offer if they are acting in pursuit of goals aimed at the corporation's long-term welfare.[28] In essence, the judgment implicitly recognized the social entity conception. Following this decision, legislative acts were passed in 28 jurisdictions in the late 1980s that in one form or another authorized a board of directors to weigh the interests of all stakeholders in their decision-making.[29] The states of Connecticut, Indiana, and Pennsylvania were especially clear in stating that directors were not obligated to give a controlling effect to any one constituency or interest. Maximizing the financial interests of shareholders was not the only core duty of a corporate director; rather directors and senior managers had to walk a tight-wire between their responsibility to investors in the form of stock market performance and to the employees and community in terms of social responsibilities.[30]

Despite this favorable legal environment, the concentrations of power in today's institutional shareholders and a highly competitive global economy have continued to exert an enormous pull on directors – pulling them towards their obligations to investors. No similar pressures remind them of the obligation to other stakeholders. As a result, most directors of publicly traded companies see shareholder value rather than social responsibility as their primary performance metric. Moreover, shareholder value can be easily and "objectively" measured by returns on equity valuations. This is not the case with contributions to a "social community" where the notion of "returns" are far more elusive in their measurement. As a result, the property conception remains the dominant one in America today. As a consequence, this paradigm of the corporation can to a large extent explain why executives and their boards in the 1980s and 1990s pegged executive compensation to shareholder returns. This in turn encouraged the exorbitant pay packages of those decades.

HOW WE CAN STRENGTHEN THE INTEGRITY OF THE EXECUTIVE COMPENSATION BARREL

Any attempt at building greater integrity in the executive compensation barrel will require a multi-pronged approach. For example, it will not be enough to rely on the self-policing efforts of boards themselves or on a set of government regulations. Moreover, compensation excess will likely be a recurring problem whenever booming equity markets appear. The temptation to profit from a boom is always great. Individuals and organizations have an enormous capacity to be "creative" when it comes to finding loopholes around existing rules and regulations or creating new means to profit from "good times." Greed is an indomitable human force, and capitalist societies are by their ideology reluctant to place serious constraints on the rights of individuals to amass wealth. That said, there have been a number of recent proposals and initiatives that can help to strengthen the integrity of the compensation barrel and restore credibility to the executive leadership of public corporations. These include: (1) full disclosure of actual compensation packages, (2) changes in the tax code, (3) changes in compensation practices themselves, and (4) shared leadership in the boardroom. We begin with the issue of transparency and the full disclosure of compensation.

Transparency for Outside Shareholders

Part of the dilemma for shareholders outside of the executive suite is a lack of detailed information on the actual compensation packages of company executives. Therefore one remedy to rein in excessive compensation would be to make that information completely transparent. Shareholders could then decide at annual meetings whether they approved of proposed compensation packages or not. In a recent *Wall Street Journal* article, Arthur Levitt, a former chairman of the SEC, offered a number of strong recommendations that could transform what is today a still opaque process into one where shareholders and the financial community could make highly informed judgments about the fairness of executive pay packages.[31] A significant first step would be for boards to disclose other forms of compensation which have been disguised to date. The use of corporate jets and automobiles, club memberships, loans, and retirement packages all need to be disclosed to shareholders. Current SEC rules do not require corporations to reveal whether compensation is performance-based and if it is, what the performance triggers are. These need to be made transparent. If the metrics for performance are changed by the board, these should be considered a critical event and therefore be fully disclosed. Levitt has suggested that corporations provide shareholders with a table that includes all benefits including perks highlighting their actual monetary value, deferred compensation, retirement benefits, and then a column that discloses the total value of compensation. These data would also be benchmarked against the same compensation metrics of their peers in the industry. If the compensation relative to performance is greater than peers, the board compensation committee would be required to provide a written justification for the difference.

Changes in the Tax Code

One vehicle to influence executive compensation through government intervention is through changes in the tax code. The current code permits corporations to deduct a "reasonable allowance for salaries and other compensation." There is no definition, however, of what constitutes "reasonable." In essence, corporations are deducting fully executive salaries, benefits, and perks as normal business expenses. There was an attempt to close this loophole through legislation in the early 1990s that capped the deductibility of executive compensation to a maximum of $1 million. But the law only capped non-performance-based salaries and so corporations passed resolutions making compensation above $1 million "performance-based" with the bulk of this in stock options and bonuses linked to performance. In 2003, new accounting regulations were passed which require that mega-grants of stock options be expensed on income statements starting in 2004. As a result, a number of public corporations such as Microsoft have dispensed completely with stock options. The Financial Accounting Standards Board has issued a new accounting standard for stock options which is supported by the Securities and Exchange Commission. This standard requires after June of 2005 that most US publicly-traded companies treat all options granted to employees as compensation expenses.[32]

That said, other forms of compensation – salaries, bonuses, restricted stock, long term payout, and assorted perks – have not come under regulatory scrutiny. As a matter of fact, the most popular alternative to stock options which are grants of restricted stock increased by 17.3 percent in 2003 to a median of $2 million at Fortune 500 companies.[33] The SEC itself has not required any major improvements in executive compensation disclosure.

Changes in Compensation Practices

As evident in this chapter, the most hotly debated dimension of the executive pay package has centered on the disbursement of stock or stock options. For example, as noted earlier, the bull market of the 1990s encouraged the widespread use of stock options as an essential part of the executive compensation package. On the one hand, this form of compensation makes great intuitive sense. After all, shareholder returns are measurable and appear to reflect the overall performance of the corporation. That said, what does compensation in equity-based rewards actually foster in terms of executive behavior?

Roger Martin of the University of Toronto argues that stock compensation by itself encourages executives to raise expectations about future, not actual, earnings since these expectations directly lead to higher stock prices. As Martin points out, there are several ways in which managers can build earnings expectations. The slowest and more difficult is to increase real earnings. The most expedient is for the CEO or CFO to hype expectations to the financial community – a popular tactic in the late 1990s. Since the fall of Enron and WorldCom, this tactic, however, has become more difficult to deploy. Wall Street is more skeptical, and financial analysts are under greater pressure to resist such hype. An additional way to inflate earnings expectations is to deploy aggressive accounting to "create" greater earnings – by filling the distribution channels to boost sales or reducing reserves for bad receivables. WorldCom, itself, supposedly classified some $7 billion in expenses as assets. A string of acquisitions can also stimulate earnings growth.[34]

Given this dilemma, Martin has proposed that boards consider abolishing stock-based compensation and in its place substitute bonuses based on real earnings. At a minimum, boards could retain stock options but ensure that they have longer vesting periods.

When it comes to stock options and rewards, Kevin Murphy notes that incentives based on options do *not* mimic the incentives of actual stock ownership despite an intuitive perception that they might.[35] They encourage only stock-price appreciation rather than total shareholder returns since total returns include dividends. Executives rewarded with options have strong incentives to avoid dividends and to prefer share repurchases. Options also have a tendency to encourage riskier investments which could dramatically increase the firm's share value. Lastly, stock options lose their incentive value when the stock price falls below the exercise price and the executive sees little chance of exercising their options. This outcome is often used as justification for repricings of options whenever there are share-price declines. In reality, stock options are at best a weak surrogate for total shareholder returns. That said, if options are employed, a more effective way to link them to share price performance would be to set their exercise price above the market price when they are issued. For example, IBM has issued its top 300 executives options with exercise prices 10 percent above the market price of the firm's stock. In the past, the company had issued them at market price.[36]

In the ideal case, companies would simply self-impose stricter compensation requirements rather than have their hands forced by changes in tax codes or government regulations. For example, in 2003, General Electric instituted a tough pay-for-performance pay plan for its CEO Jeffrey Immelt. He was granted 250,000 "performance share units" (each unit is equivalent to a share of stock in value) which at the time had a market value of $7.5 million. He receives half of them if he is able to grow GE's total shareholder return so that it meets or beats the S&P 500's returns between 2003 and 2007. He receives the other half if he grows GE's operating cash flow by 10 percent a year during that same period.[37]

In addition to the compensation of the executives themselves, any reform in current practices would need to address board director compensation. In research by Donal Byard and Ying Li on executive pay, it was discovered that a heavier reliance on stock options as compensation for independent board directors more tightly aligned their behavior to the interests of top management rather than shareholders.[38] For example, they found that the granting of options involved greater timing opportunism when directors on the compensation committee received a greater proportion of stock options in their compensation package. Timing opportunism involves the ability to profit relatively quickly from the granting of options by issuing them either just before positive news or just after bad news. This problem is compounded by the fact that a significant percentage of director compensation is now in stock options. It may be time to return to director compensation without options, or else option arrangements that are structured to preclude timing opportunism. For example, timing opportunism might be addressed by spreading option grants to the CEO over the course of a year in equal monthly installments versus the current practice of a single grant once a year.[39]

Lastly, it is important to reconsider the "performance standards" that are employed for compensation decisions. For example, the primary determinant for bonuses is accounting profits. However, as Kevin Murphy notes, there are two dilemmas with this metric. Accounting profits are inherently backward-looking and short term. Executives can enhance accounting profits with actions that harm the long-term profitability of the firm. For example, they may cut R&D spending or manipulate profits shifting earnings across periods or adjustments in accruals. Performance standards based on budgets or prior-year performance can create additional problems. It is possible to "sandbag" the budget process or simply promote incremental performance improvements to beat last year's performance. Generally speaking, external performance standards are more objective measures – for example standards based on the cost of capital or standards based on the performance of an industry peer group.[40]

Boardroom Leadership Remedies

Though the idea of a separate or non-executive boardroom chair has been circulating around for at least a decade, only a small minority of companies have adopted the idea. The slow inroads made by the practice suggest strong resistance to the idea. This, however, has not stopped governance commissions and activist pension funds from promoting the idea. In its study of board best practices, the Blue Ribbon Commission on Director Professionalism, a prestigious 28-member group created by the National Association of Corporate Directors and headed by noted governance specialist Ira Millstein, concluded: "Boards should consider formally designating a non-executive chairman or other independent board leader." An equally high-profile group, the Committee on Corporate Governance in Canada, sponsored by the Toronto Stock Exchange, made a similar recommendation: "In our view, the board should be able to function independently of management . . . Perhaps the simplest means for implementing this guideline is for the board to appoint a strong non-executive chair of the board whose principal responsibility is managing the board of directors."[41]

The principal arguments in favor of a separate or non-executive chair have to do with enhancing the ability of the board to monitor the CEO's performance and leadership. It is assumed that directors will feel more at ease to raise challenges to the CEO if the board is led by a fellow director. In addition, fund managers often assume that a CEO seeks first to serve themselves and secondarily the shareholders. A non-executive chair whose mandate is to enhance shareholder value is less likely to be compromised.

There is one important caveat to this suggestion. If the separate board chair is *a former CEO* of the firm, then there is not a genuine independent and objective counter-balance to the CEO since the chairperson is most likely to have chosen the CEO him/herself. A CEO whose board chair is the company's former CEO describes the dilemma:

> If he [the board chair] has been involved in selecting the new guy to be CEO as was true in my case, the chair is in a kind of funny position of not being able to be critical of the new guy for some time. He's got to preserve the honeymoon aspect of it. If a new guy comes in and wants to change anything, there is also the unavoidable

explicit criticism of the old guy insofar as how he did things. There is an awkward tension set up between the new guy and the old guy that results in an awful lot of senatorial dancing around the issue of why these problems existed before and why the old guy didn't do anything about them. If the new guy comes in and wants to dramatically change direction, he has the old guy who is lurking there either biting his tongue or, heaven forbid, arguing with him about it. If the new guy wants to kill some of the pet projects of the old guy, it is an awkward situation. Personally, I believe the retiring CEO is "in the way" in the simplest of terms and should go out gracefully. If the new CEO wants to call on the wisdom of the retired CEO he is certainly free to do that without the old guy being on the board.[42]

It is important, therefore, that the board chair not be someone who is the former CEO. As importantly, it must be an individual who is highly admired by the directors themselves and who has the self-confidence and industry knowledge to take a leadership role especially during times of trouble. They must also be someone who can be dedicated to following both the company and the industry closely. In addition, the non-executive chairperson should not hold board directorships elsewhere given the role's potentially high demands. Nor should the company's CEO sit on the chair's board if the chair him/herself is a CEO. In general, however, standing CEOs of other companies are not appropriate given the normal demands on their time as a standing CEO of another organization. With this form of counter-balancing board leadership, the system of "checks and balances" is further reinforced when it comes to abuses in the area of executive compensation.

CONCLUSION

In the ideal world, boards would take it upon themselves to impose stricter means of both evaluating and rewarding executive compensation. Government regulations also need to play a role in the process. Sarbanes Oxley is one such step in that direction. Finally, shareholders must become more active participants or at the least overseers of executive compensation practices. Pension funds with their longer term investment horizons and large holdings in individual companies have the greatest incentive to reshape executive compensation. One would also hope that executives would themselves come to appreciate how perceptions of excessive compensation have hurt their own credibility as leaders. A greater degree of restraint on their part will go a long way to enhance public perceptions. There is some reason to be hopeful. A recent survey of 2004 compensation data for CEOs of large US companies shows a rise of just 5 percent compared with increases of 7.2 percent in 2003 and 10 percent in 2002.[43] This is very promising news in light of the fact that 2004 appears to be one of the most profitable years for US corporations.

Moreover, there is a continued shift away from option schemes towards restricted stock awards. We may be in a transition period at the end of which executive compensation levels may come back to earth.

NOTES

1. Boyle, M. (2004), 2003 Executive Compensation, *Fortune*, vol. 149, issue 9, page 123, May 3.
2. Ibid.
3. Steward, J. (2003), Spend! Spend! Spend!, *The New Yorker*, Feb. 17 and 24, pp. 132–47.
4. Clark, K. (2003), At the Center of the Corporate Scandal: Where Do We Go from Here? Presentation to the National Press Club, Feb. 26.
5. Arbogast, G., Grundig, J., Peirano, L., and Dayton, T. (2002), CEO Compensation Versus Performance: A Qualitative Analysis, paper presented to the Academy of Business Disciplines, Fort Myers Beach, FL, November.
6. Ibid.
7. Walcott, J. (2004) Today's College Freshmen Party Less, Volunteer More. Christian Science Monitor, online edition retrieved from http://www,csmonitor.com/2004/0203/p14s01-legn.htm
8. Conger, J.A., Lawler, E.E., and Finegold, D. (2001), *Corporate Boards: New Strategies for Adding Value at the Top*, San Francisco, CA: Jossey-Bass.
9. Binmore, K. (1994), *Playing Fair*, Cambridge, MA and London: The MIT Press.
10. Levitt, A. (2004), Money, Money, Money, *The Wall Street Journal*, Nov. 22, p. A14.
11. Clark, op. cit.
12. Ibid.
13. Arbogast, G., et al., op. cit., p. 3.
14. Bizjak, J.M., Lemmon, M.L., and Naveen, L. (2000), Has the Use of Peer Groups Contributed to Higher Levels of Executive Compensation? Working Paper, Department of Finance, Portland State University.
15. Meindl, J.R., Ehrlich, S.B. and Dukerich, J.M. (1985), The Romance of Leadership, *Administrative Science Quarterly*, 30, 521–51.
16. Yukl, G. (1994), *Leadership in Organizations* (3rd edn), Englewood Cliffs, NJ: Prentice Hall.
17. Meindl et al., op. cit.
18. Maccoby, M. (2000), Narcissistic Leaders: The Incredible Pros, the Inevitable Cons, *Harvard Business Review*, Jan–Feb, pp. 69–77.
19. Ibid. p. 75.
20. Steward, J. (2003), p. 137.
21. Allen, W.T. (1992, April 13), Our Schizophrenic Conception of the Business Corporation, Paper presented to the Samuel and Ronnie Heyman Center on Corporate Governance, Cardozo School of Law, Yeshiva University, New York. Published in *The Cardozo Law Review*, 1992, 14, 261 and retrieved from electronic database.
22. Ibid.
23. Ibid.
24. Ibid.
25. Ibid.
26. Ibid.
27. Ibid.
28. Ibid.
29. Ibid.
30. Ibid.
31. Levitt, A. (2004), Money, Money, Money, *Wall Street Journal*, Nov. 22, page A14.
32. *Financial Times* (2004), Tougher Options, December 20, p. 16.

33. Boyle, M., op. cit.
34. Martin, R. (January 1, 2003), Taking Stock, *Harvard Business Review*, p. 34.
35. Murphy, K. (1999), Executive Compensation, Working Paper, Marshall School of Business, University of Southern California, p.18.
36. *Financial Times* (2004), op. cit., p.16.
37. Boyle, M. (2004), 2003 Executive Compensation Report, *Fortune*, May 3, vol. 149, issue 9, p. 123.
38. Morgenson, G. (2004), Are Options Seducing Directors Too?, *New York Times*, Dec. 12, p. 1 (section 3).
39. Ibid., p. 4.
40. Murphy, K., op. cit.
41. Conger, Lawler, and Finegold, op. cit.
42. Ibid.
43. Roberts, D. (2004), Chief Executives Stem Rises in Their Salaries to Avoid Embarrassment, *Financial Times*, Dec. 13, p. 1.

6. Dirty hands, necessary sin, and the ethics of leaders

Peter Temes

I spent part of 2003 and 2004 talking to audiences about Just War theory, the subject of a book that I'd recently written and, of course, the subject of much national debate before and during the American invasion of Iraq. My book covered a lot of ground, and early on I wasn't sure which of its points of emphasis would be the most engaging when I got up to speak – maybe the arguments for or against pure pacifism, or about the role of the UN in national policy making. As it turned out, neither got that much traction. To my surprise, people were much more interested in the abstract idea of "Necessary Sin" that I tried to explain in the book, a variation on the classical philosophical dilemma of "Dirty Hands."

One of the central notions of my book was that war is always wrong, but sometimes necessary. That is, we cannot say that intentional killing and destruction as a matter of policy is in any way good. By any moral principle worth defending, these are bad acts. Bad as they are, though, from the perspective of national policy, they are at times the least bad among a finite set of options. A head of state enters his or her moment of decision-making about war with all of the constraints inherited from years, decades, and centuries of other leaders' decisions – all of their mistakes, all of their moral shortcomings, all of their compromises with forces they deemed insuperable. To say, as a social critic might rightly say, "this war is the result of two decades of bad decisions," is important for everyone except for the decision maker in the time of crisis, choosing among available options rather than among what *might* have been possible had a head of state zigged instead of zagged in 1948, or 1958, or even five years ago.

For the pacifist, this is not a meaningful moral dilemma, for by definition the pacifist will choose to suffer any harm – and worse (in my opinion), will choose to have others suffer any harm – before seeing war as necessary. But from any other perspective we can see that in the middle of the progress of history, war is indeed sometimes the least bad option. We might say that the Second World War, for example, so often seen as the touchstone of "good" wars, was itself a terrible moral failure. Had better decisions been made in

1929, in 1938, in 1939, and on and on, we might well have found alternatives to the world conflagration. But those better decisions were not made.

Imagine yourself a world leader – a Roosevelt, a Churchill – and let us even grant that you feel the decisions made by your predecessors were terrible ones, that war might have been avoided had they been better. There you are in your own moment, forced to deal with the world as it is. If you choose war, you choose a bad thing. But in that moment, any alternative is worse. This is the "Necessary Sin" of the leader in a time of war, and the idea certainly struck a resonant chord as the Bush administration began our second war in Iraq.

It is a variation on the classic philosophical dilemma of Dirty Hands, of the leader doing some dirty work to help the group. My understanding of the Dirty Hands dilemma is that it is broader than what I have called Necessary Sin, and often involves a greater sense of self-justification. That is, I imagine the Dirty Hands leader seeing his hands as dirty but his conscience as clean, because he is delivering the goods to the group. I imagine the Necessary Sin leader understanding the moral failure he or she undertakes, feeling no better option, and seeking to forestall worse events, rather than choosing the stain of dirt because of a forward-looking expectation of gain.

Jean-Paul Sartre's play "Dirty Hands" (*Les Mains Sales*), illustrates the concept well. In it, a Communist fighter tries to shake a younger man out of his foolish idealism, the kind of idealism that, it seems, paralyzes men in those rare moments when fleeting acts of violence might bring victory to their causes. Sartre's character feels the younger man is exercising a kind of selfishness by thinking in moral terms. What is needed, instead, is an unsentimental dedication to getting things done to further the revolution. The older man says to the idealist:

> How you cling to your purity, young man! How afraid you are to soil your hands! All right, stay pure! What good will it do? Purity is an idea for a yogi or a monk. You intellectuals and bourgeois anarchists use it as a pretext for doing nothing. To do nothing, to remain motionless, arms at your sides, wearing kid gloves. Well, I have dirty hands. Right in to the elbows. You don't love men. . . . You love only principles. Your purity resembles death.

Sartre offers even more layers of complexity than this bit of dialogue suggests. The older man is about to strike a deal with right-wing forces to join in a joint bid to seize power. His group might well win, in that they will share great power, but at the same time they will lose, in that they will not be seizing power *as communists*, but as compromisers with their most explicit enemies. At the same time, the young man has been sent to see the older man not to negotiate with him, but to kill him, to keep the communist forces out of the alliance with the right-wingers. So if the older man wins his argument with the younger man, and convinces him to abandon his scruples and to act instead of thinking so much, the young man will certainly carry out his orders and kill the older man.

The first apparent meaning of the Dirty Hands dilemma here, then, is that to act decisively in service to a cause you must, like the older man, accept the dirt that stains those who get things done. But the second apparent meaning seems to cancel the first – it seems to suggest that once one accepts the Dirty Hands principle, one cannot argue. The Dirty Hands position takes one entirely out of the business of applying ideas to the world and acting with any sense of consistency beyond brute self-interest. The very idea that one can see one's hands as dirty suggests a moral consciousness, though it is a moral consciousness strong enough to make a judgment (these hands are dirty) yet not strong enough to determine action, to keep those hands clean. Some philosophers see this as an appropriate compromise between idealism and the necessary compromises of social action.[1] Because of this self-canceling second meaning of the Dirty Hands principle, the concept of Necessary Sin seems perhaps especially useful, because it allows the actor to hold on to moral reflection and logical argument for a moment longer, even if at the cost of a much greater sense of self-revulsion.

The phrase itself invites a certain amount of trouble, though. First, the word "sin" brings with it the obvious religious context, something that many audiences don't expect but find meaningful. To discuss sin rather than, say, "moral culpability," is to presume some kind of agreement about what sin is. In fact, this use of the word "sin" draws on a commonly accepted notion of doing wrong, without building a careful construct that limits the notion to a time, place, faith tradition, or other context. Many will respond by saying, Yes, that is precisely the problem with this word – it encourages an unthinking sense of wrong, and avoids precisely the kind of thinking out loud that we must do to create a meaningful context for moral discussion. This use of "sin" does the easy work of offering judgment but avoids the hard work of discussing the history packed into the word, the layered complications of hundreds – even thousands – of years of religious practice and malpractice.

Which is entirely true. Yet the complexity of context seems to argue against the usefulness of the core idea – the more we add nuance to a word that serves to anchor our moral calculus at one extreme (in this case, if "sin" is too simple, imagine if we were to use the word "bad" in its place), the less able we are to act based on the principle we are creating. The task at hand, then, is to find an ethical principle simple enough that we can use it toward some good end, but nuanced enough that we do not become moral clods, pronouncing judgment rather than reasoning well. That seems a fine challenge for Leadership Studies as a discipline.

Philosopher Harry Frankfurt has made the important distinction between what he calls first-order and second-order will – that is, between a person's will to do something (first-order) and a reflection on that will, in a sense his will to *have* that will.[2] At the first order, I might want to eat some ice cream. That's my desire, or my appetite. At the second order, I reflect on this desire, and I say to myself, eating ice cream under these conditions is a fine thing. I accept and approve of my own desire. I might even be motivated more by the second order, and say to myself, on a day like today, a person in my position really should want to have some ice cream, so I will cultivate that desire.

Frankfurt's distinction becomes less a parlor-room exercise when we apply it to social and political leadership. I might want wealth or power as a matter of my first-order appetites, but as a matter of second-order reflection, I might tell myself that those are not good desires in my place and time. Or I might look around and say, under these conditions, a good person would want to help others, and find my motive for the will to help at that second level rather than emerging as an appetite. The reflective individual operates at both levels Frankfurt identifies, and the second-level reflection ought, one imagines, to enable more ethical action in the long run.

Frankfurt's distinction is generally presented in a positive manner, with the reflective individual judging his or her desire on the basis of what is most right. Another application, of course, is for the individual to judge his desires on the basis of what is least wrong, and here we re-enter the consideration of Dirty Hands and Necessary Sin.

Necessary Sin is second-order thinking – the leader is aware that she should not and does not want the burden of a certain act, but recognizes that this act is necessary for the sake of the group. That second-order self-consciousness deepens the sacrifice of the leader, and enlarges the scale of the leader's contribution to the group. Not only is the leader making a sacrifice for the group, the leader is knowingly sacrificing her sense of being someone who does good acts instead of bad acts. It is with this second order of will in mind that we can begin to see the profound dimension of the burden of leadership in times of crisis.

But this idea of Frankfurt's raises another important question. A new wrinkle is added to the basic moral challenge of leadership – how to tell right from wrong, and then help make right happen. With Necessary Sin in mind, now we have to ask what the limits on that sin might be. Are we supposing that Frankfurt's second-order self-consciousness is so blunt that once the line is crossed and the leader does something he knows to be wrong for the sake of the group, that all moral claims are released, that all things on the other side of the moral divide are equally bad?[3] Are we saying that the leader who feels no choice but to lie or to steal for the sake of the group is doing nothing different from killing thousands for the sake of the group? I presume not. And so we now have at least three categories of moral consideration: what is right, what is wrong, and what is wrong but not too wrong for the leader to fit in the category of Necessary Sin. This third category is of course the hardest to grasp, and this is where tools of moral judgment are most vitally needed.

THREE IDEAS FOR THINKING ABOUT THE ETHICS OF LEADERSHIP

Here are three examples of ethical thinking that might be useful for leaders to use when they think about ethics. The idea here is to offer a way to talk about matters of leadership that makes central the question of toward what end, not merely how or with what effect.

First Idea: Defining the Good

Jeremy Bentham and John Stuart Mill offered classic definitions of utilitarianism, though of course they disagreed with each other.[4,5] Beginning with the proposition that good leadership delivers the greatest good for the greatest number, Bentham defined "good" in terms of happiness, while Mill defined good in terms of "well-being."[6] Happiness is of course a subjective state – whether I am happy is entirely up to me. Well-being is another matter entirely. One might look at a man sleeping in his own filth in the street who declares with a full heart "I am happy" yet still be gravely concerned for his well-being. Rather like Just War theory, which requires that we answer questions like "is this war being waged by a legitimate authority," but does not define "legitimate," utilitarianism offers ethical questions but not decisive answers.

Still, to be asking these questions – to see that ethical leadership is as much about the difference between leadership that delivers happiness and leadership that delivers well-being – is to invite fundamental philosophical questions that are too often left out of the discussion today.

Students of leadership can benefit from grappling with some of the classical attempts to make meaningful distinctions between happiness and well-being. Plato's Allegory of the Cave, from *The Republic*, is an excellent starting point.

Plato's allegory describes a world in which people sit inside a cave, never venturing out, watching images projected on the cave's back wall all day long. A large fire burns on a high ledge behind the people, and puppeteers stand in front of the flames with their puppets. This is Plato's rendering of the scene, in Alan Bloom's translation:

> See human beings as though they were in an underground cave-like dwelling with its entrance, a long one, open to the light across the whole width of the cave. They are in it from childhood with their legs and necks in bonds so that they are fixed, seeing only in front of them, unable because of the bond to turn their heads

all the way around. Their light is from a fire burning far above and behind them. Between the fire and the prisoners there is a road above, along which see a wall, built like the partitions puppet-handlers set in front of the human beings and over which they show the puppets. (Book 7, section 515)

The images on the cave wall that captivate everyone are about as close an equivalent to modern television as a man living in the fourth century BC could imagine.

Plato asks, what would happen if a man were able to escape from this cave, and see the true sun rather than the reflected images of a fire? What if he were to see the rest of the world outside the cave, instead of only shadowed images? Well, Plato tell us through his character Socrates, he would go mad.

But what if somehow he managed to survive his raw encounter with the real, and then returned to the cave to tell the others about the unimaginably great world outside the cave – and about how pale an imitation of reality their sad cave-bound existence truly is? What would happen to this truth-teller? Plato tells us that he would be killed by the others in the cave. They would not be able to stand the thought of living without their illusions.

The cave-dwellers are happy. They have calibrated their desires and appetites to meet the narrow world of their cave, and upsetting that balance is frightening to them. But certainly they do not enjoy a state of well-being. Their lives are stunted, their imaginations atrophied and their will effectively vanquished. One might argue that it is better to lose one's life in service to the truth than to live happily within a lie. That is, the truth-teller who is killed by the group experiences more well-being in his fleeting moment of knowledge of the real world and his noble attempt to shake his comrades out of their collective stupor than he would have experienced in the rest of his life as a cave-dweller. Best of all, of course, would be for the truth-teller to have found a more effective strategy to make the change he sought – to bring a greater amount of well-being to a greater number of people.

The questions for leadership studies here are vitally important, and this exercise offers a productive joining of the abstract – what is the difference between happiness and well-being – with the tactical – how could the truth-teller in Plato's cave have been more effective. One hopes that the connections between these two questions – and these two planes of questioning – can become a central part of the study of leadership.

Second Idea: What Matters Is . . .

To go beyond ethical questioning to ethical answering, philosopher Peter Singer in his recent writings on economic globalization offers this decisive statement: "What matters is people's welfare, not the size of the gap between rich and poor."[7] This is an explicit tool for evaluating claims of the fairness of economic structures and arrangements. Singer locates the moral value of these structures and arrangements in what they do for individuals, rather than how they affect relations among larger groups. One might easily argue the opposing position, but Singer's statement offers a moral frame of the most explicit clarity in a manner that is directly relevant – and in my opinion morally useful – for understanding, and for playing the role of leader, in the world today.

Singer's moral logic begins with a presumption that the moral goodness of a society is best measured by the material state of its poorest members. From this perspective one might propose that in the US, for example, globalization reveals its morally bad nature because the poorest of the poor in the US are, from some perspectives, hurt economically by being forced to compete economically with even poorer workers in other countries – that globalization draws us into a "race to the bottom." And this might be true if the US were in any sense a complete and total society, that is, if we were able to think about social ethics only within the frame of our own country, without reference or regard to the larger frame of other nations, peoples and places. Singer's point – revealed in the title of his book *One World* – is that the US is not a complete and total society, and no nation is. Instead, in our age, there is only one society, and that is the global human society. In our age, we cannot think about the effects of social policies or market dynamics only in terms of Americans, or only in terms of Canadians, or only in terms of Zambians. The interconnection of all nations we witness in our world today demands that we consider the experience of people everywhere before we judge the moral adequacy of any social policy or market dynamic.

From that perspective, we can see that while globalization might make a factory worker in the US poorer (itself an arguable statement), that individual loses less than the new factory worker in, say, eastern China or northern Mexico gains. Looking at the world as one community, and applying Singer's admirably clear principle of judgment, ethical thinking can operate usefully. We might say that Singer's tool is a bad tool, or that it is poorly applied, and thus offer alternative principles and applications of them to the world, but the equation here – from moral principle to application to conclusion about the world – is essential if we are to use philosophy productively in understanding the world and then helping to change it in a positive manner.

Third Idea: Where Morality Functions

To reach one level higher from Singer's statement – to go from the level of moral assertion to a moral principle expressed in that assertion – I would propose this meta-statement: morality functions at the level of the individual, not the level of the group. True or not, this statement is a tool for making explicit judgments and to motivate action, with a clear moral frame.

To offer a personal example that should resonate for others in the business of higher education, one of my roles as the head of a graduate school is to participate in decision-making at my university, and to lead decision-making within my graduate school, about issues of diversity. The issues of diversity on campus are some of the most challenging and important that any academic community can face. Yet we seldom manage to engage these issues within an explicit moral frame. Instead, much of the dialogue in higher education revolves around what is permissible and what is mandated by law, and around a general sense of the good of diversity in and of itself. So when we address issues like scholarship programs targeted to create and support more racial and ethnic diversity on campus, the questions "how can we do this," "how will it be received on campus," and "what are the legal and policy limitations we'll face" tend to be central. Questions like, "Is this morally right" are seldom asked, perhaps because there is an assumption of consensus on that point, an assumption built, in my opinion, on a false sense of the moral question's simplicity. As a case in point, in a conversation with undergraduate students demanding a series of changes to the student life programs at their school, when I asked one student one of the questions I thought foundational to the discussion of diversity and race-conscious programs at colleges – is the best response to unfairness a counter-balancing unfairness, or fairness itself? – she rejected the question as overly philosophical, while I take that question to be essential to guide me in doing the things I do as a practical administrator.

If the test of morality is how a given action or policy affects individuals rather than groups – and, therefore, if one can find an action or policy immoral because one can find the individual example of the person it harms unfairly – then we wind up needing to take specific positions when we address race and diversity on campus. On my campus, for example, about a year ago we began a new scholarship program aimed at creating and supporting greater racial and ethnic diversity among our student body. The goal of the program was explicit, to bring more students of color to our campus and to support more academic work that served poor communities. Putting aside the moving target of federal policy on these matters, the most direct path for us to take on this matter would have been to designate scholarship funds for students of color. Yet this would violate the principle that morality functions at the level of the individual, because though this approach would serve the group-level ends we had in mind quite effectively, it would also allow the case of one student being told, in effect, you cannot have this support because of your racial identity. We could help (in a small way) lessen injustice at the group level by imposing new injustice at the level of the individual – not an acceptable position passed on the foundational principle. So we specifically built into our program that racial identity is not a test, and further said that any student whose presence helped serve the larger goals of the program would be eligible. In the end, out of 30 recipients of the scholarship in its first year, three were not students of color by any measure, and their presence has not only enhanced the program through the particulars of the work and ideas of these three people, but it has also made our program a better one from a moral perspective, *if* one holds (as I do) that foundational principle, that morality functions at the level of the individual more than at the level of the group.

In the case of the diversity scholarship fund, we found a tool for ethical thinking that worked well for our purposes, at least from my perspective as an institutional leader. I fear, though, that it is only the practical scale of the challenge – one policy at one institution – that allowed that resolution. The more at stake, the less effective our ethical tools are likely to be – but, therefore, the more important the work to craft such tools will be, because the unmet need is so great. Consider, again, the fundamental question of war and peace. From a moral perspective, we can easily recognize that war is in many ways bad, and that peace is in many ways good. And I am certainly tempted to say flatly that war is worse than peace – and to apply this principle by saying, given a choice, choose peace over war in every case. But if we consider the fullness of time, we find that choosing peace today might bring more harm tomorrow than today's war. And so the ethical equation must become far more complex than "X is better than Y, so choose X." Open-ended qualifications become necessary – "X is better than Y to the extent that X will not lead to more Y later."

The case of Neville Chamberlain is a good illustration. By 1938, Germany had fully emerged from its post-First World War humiliation. With Adolph Hitler as its head of state, a strong and aggressive military, and broad civilian support for aggression across its borders, Germany threatened that September to invade Czechoslovakia. The Czech army was actually quite strong, and if it had been backed by British and French forces, it might have fought off Hitler and weakened the Nazi regime in the process. So Hitler needed to isolate Czechoslovakia, to pull a strand apart from the nominal alliance of the Czechs, the British, and the French. With a victory against an isolated Czechoslovakia, he could then continue on to the British and the French, left without their former ally, and thus no longer a match to the German military machine. Neville Chamberlain, then Prime Minister of England, has been remembered as a tragic figure because he chose the short-term ideal of peace over what virtually all later observers have seen as the ugly but necessary commitment to join with France and Czechoslovakia to fight Germany. That war would have brought with it some of the horror that began unfolding a year later, after Hitler invaded Poland (having taken all of Czechoslovakia earlier) and the rest of Europe understood that the world war had begun, but would have likely made of Hitler a militarist more on the scale of Slobodan Milosovic or Saddam

Hussein – dangerous, murderous, but blocked from his fantasy of broad empire. But that was not the path chosen by Neville Chamberlain.

Duff Cooper, then England's First Lord of the Admiralty and author of the war memoir *Old Men Forget*, wrote about Chamberlain's report to the British Cabinet on the notorious Munich Agreement, signed by Chamberlain, French prime minister Edouard Daladier, Adolph Hitler and Benito Mussolini, ceding the heart of Czechoslovakia to Germany.

> The Prime Minister looked none the worse for his experiences. He spoke for over an hour. He told us that Hitler had adopted a certain position for the start and had refused to budge an inch from it. . . . [T]he prime minister concluded, to my astonishment, by saying that he considered that we should accept those terms and that we should advise the Czechs to do so. It was then suggested that the cabinet should adjourn, in order to give members time to read the terms and sleep on them, and that we should meet again the following morning. I protested against this. I said that from what the Prime Minister had told us it appeared to me that the Germans were still convinced that under no circumstances would we fight, that there still existed one method, and one method only, of persuading them to the contrary, and that was by instantly declaring full mobilisation.[8]

But Chamberlain was determined to avoid war, at almost any cost. On the 30th of September, 1938, he issued a joint statement with Hitler about the Munich Agreement. It read, in part: "We regard the agreement signed last night and the Anglo-German Naval Agreement as symbolic of the desire of our two peoples never to go to war with one another again."[9] Peace is so precious, and war so ugly. Yet in this case, the years that followed made it stunningly clear that, as John Stuart Mill had written 80 years earlier, though war is almost unthinkably awful, some things are worse than war. It is the burden of the head of state, the general, and the policy planner to choose between the things worse than war and war itself, and at times to say to citizens "we must fight." That is not what Chamberlain said in a radio broadcast on September 27th, three days before his joint announcement with Hitler. Instead, he had this to say to his countrymen:

> How horrible, fantastic, incredible, it is that we should be digging trenches and trying on gas-masks here because of a quarrel in a far-away country between people of whom we know nothing! I would not hesitate to pay even a third visit to Germany, if I thought it would do any good.

> Armed conflict between nations is a nightmare to me; but if I were convinced that any nation had made up its mind to dominate the world by fear of its force, I should feel that it must be resisted. Under such a domination, life for people who believe in liberty would not be worth living; but war is a fearful thing, and we must be very clear, before we embark on it, that it is really the great issues that are stake.[10]

While waiting for further clarity, Chamberlain and Daladier chose to cede the Sudetenland of Czechoslovakia to Hitler, to chose an unjust peace over a war that might have done a great deal of good and forestalled the deaths of millions, the crushing of a dozen national governments, and the advent of industrial genocide.

So here is the challenge: how do we frame an ethical principle that, applied to the choices Chamberlain faced, will yield the morally best result? The tradition of Just War thinking is the answer to this question that has unfolded over several centuries. It takes the complex form mentioned above – "X is better than Y to the extent that X will not lead to more Y later." Thus Just War teachings going back as far as Augustine say that "the purpose of war is peace." And a central principle of the Just War tradition is the notion of proportionality, the idea that the harm done by war be less than the good done by the peace that follows.

This language about war can easily seem hypocritical, and it demands enough interpretation by the reader that it certainly can be a tool for justifying wars that will be fought regardless of Just War questions. Yet the Just War tradition offers leaders important ethical insights for making positive change in the world – whether that change be bringing a bad war to an early end, or bringing a tyrant to his knees. The tools for this change are ideas – ethical ideas. With the courage to debate and apply these ideas of right and wrong, educators can make perhaps the most important of contributions that the academy is able to foster – the development of moral leaders for the future. Without that courage, scholars and teachers will have more to say to each other than to the world.

NOTES

1. Michael Walzer's essay "Political Action: the Problem of Dirty Hands" takes this position, applauding the guilty consciences of figures in authority who do the bad deeds they feel they must do. Without their feelings of guilt, they'd do even more bad things; with yet stronger feelings of guilt, they'd be paralyzed in the face of crises that require action. Yet there is a cynicism at the base of this position, in applauding the retraining effects of moral feelings, but not acknowledging the demands of those moral feelings in their own terms, that is, in terms of prescribing what one ought not to do. Walzer's argument leaves him far closer than he would like to thinkers like Leo Strauss, who wishes the masses to embrace religion because religious feelings lead them to better social behavior, though Strauss sees religion as bunk.
2. The best resource for understanding Frankfurt's ideas about will is his collection of essays, *The Importance of What We Care About*, Cambridge: Cambridge University Press, 1988.
3. Some quite important thinkers do seem to say this; Michael Walzer's notion of "emergency ethics" is a stark example. See Walzer's *Just and Unjust Wars*, New York: Basic Books, 1977.
4. Mill's 1863 book *Utilitarianism* is an essential source for understanding his position. Bentham's 1789 *Introduction to the Principles of Morals and Legislation* is the central text for understanding his position.

5. Bloom's translation, with commentary, was published by Basic Books in New York in 1968.

6. As Joanne Ciulla has pointed out, Mill arrives at "well-being" as the logical extension of the happiness that people seek in their daily lives, following the logical chain that Aristotle first presented in his *Nicomacian Ethics*. Mill himself might object to this dualism between his well-being and Bentham's happiness, proposing like Aristotle that the connection between happiness and virtue, or happiness and well-being, is obvious. That is, he might say that he is not arguing against Bentham, but instead taking Bentham to the next level.

7. The argument is found in Singer's book *One World: The Ethics of Globalization*, New Haven, CT: Yale University Press, 2002.

8. Duff Cooper's *Old Men Forget* was published by Rupert Hart-Davis in London, in 1953. The passage above was cited at http://www.spartacus.schoolnet.co.uk/2WWmunich.htm

9. The Brigham Young "EuroDocs" project offers this and related texts at http://www.lib.byu.edu/~rdh/eurodocs/uk/peace.html

10. For the full text of this speech and related comment, see Larry William Fuchser's *Neville Chamberlain and Appeasement: A Study in the Politics of History*, New York: W.W. Norton, 1982.

PART THREE

The body of leadership:
moral systems and organizations

7. Fairness as effectiveness: how leaders lead

Tom R. Tyler

Let me begin by referring to recent surveys assessing American workers' opinions of managerial ethics. In one study, American workers viewed the ethical nature of leader conduct as playing a key role in shaping their overall opinions of their leaders. In another study, Watson Wyatt Employee Attitudes and Opinions Survey finds that many employees question the ethics of management, with 44 percent indicating that the top management of their company is not honest.[1] Here, dishonesty refers to hypocrisy, not criminal conduct. Although these numbers seem relatively high in comparison to other surveys,[2] they still underscore the widespread finding that many employees are concerned about the ethical conduct of higher-level managers.

The Watson Wyatt survey group manager, Ilene Gochman, suggests that these employee concerns about management ethics spell trouble for management, since "[o]ne of the biggest drivers in commitment to the company is trust in senior management."[3] Consistent with this argument, other survey results suggest that many employees would like to leave their current jobs. In fact, one survey shows widespread employee discontent with the climate in their current workplace, with estimates that eight out of ten workers are planning to look for a new job when the economy improves.[4] The results of these surveys are consistent with a familiar theme in management – that the ethical climate of workplaces matters to employees.[5] That argument is supported by experimental evidence that workers are less satisfied with workplaces characterized by injustice, less productive in such settings, and more likely to leave them.[6]

I highlight these findings because they are consistent with a theme that emerges in my recent research on employees' behavior in work settings and that will be the focus of my chapter. Since I am a psychologist, this research approaches leadership from a behavioral point of view. The theme that emerges from empirical research on leadership is that the perceived ethical character of managers has a strong influence on the degree to which employees commit to the company, follow work rules, and adhere to ethical guidelines. As a consequence, I suggest that leaders must be seen as acting justly by those they lead if they wish to be effective in managing those within their organizations. While ethicists emphasize that leaders must be ethical to be legitimate, my work focuses on the argument that leaders must be seen by their followers as being ethical if they are to be effective.

The literature to which I refer involves the study of how leaders motivate their followers. It views the ability to motivate desirable behavior on the part of group members as a key feature of effective leadership.[7] The ability to motivate employees has always been one important component of leadership in work organizations, but this issue has taken on a new importance in recent years in the wake of corporate scandals. It has become increasingly important to understand how leaders can motivate ethical behavior on the part of group members. Leaders, in other words, are recognized as being the key in efforts to create an ethical work climate. They need to be able to motivate their followers to behave ethically by following organizational rules.

To create an ethical work climate, an organization must have ethically based rules and policies as well as widespread adherence among organizational members. Such adherence is difficult to achieve, since members of an organization may break rules to satisfy their immediate self-interests without regard to the damage done to the interests of the larger group. Whether the behavior is stealing office supplies or violating accounting rules, rule breaking can lead to immediate gains for the rule breaker. Hence, leaders must be able to motivate their followers to put the interests of the group above their own immediate self-interest. People need to be willing to follow rules even when those rules do not maximize their personal self-interest.

So, leaders need first to be ethical and to work to create an organization that has rules and policies that are consistent with ethical procedures. They then need to have the ability to motivate their followers to adhere to those rules and policies, even when policy adherence requires that followers do not act in ways that maximize their personal self-interest. It is to the latter issue that my comments are directed. In recent corporate scandals one problem has been that leaders have lacked ethical values and have engaged in unethical conduct. This issue is not addressed in this chapter, since such leaders are unlikely to be motivated to try to create an ethical workplace. Rather, this chapter is directed toward the situation in which leaders are ethical and are seeking to create a climate within which the employees in their work organization follow ethical principles.

WHAT MOTIVATES EMPLOYEES?

One factor shaping employee motivation is the perceived procedural justice of the workplace. Procedural justice judgments are employee assessments of the fairness or unfairness of the processes by which leaders exercise their authority. This includes both the policies and practices of an organization and the actions of particular authorities when making and implementing particular policies and decisions. We can best understand the issue of procedural justice by comparing it to alternative psychological models. One way that people might be shaped by their organization is in reaction to the resources leaders provide. We can look at this either in terms of the intrinsic favorability of outcomes or by reference to the contingency that people see between incentives and performance (virtue is rewarded), sanctions and rule adherence (transgression is punished). In either case, the basic suggestion is that employee behavior is shaped by the resources that the organization provides to support adherence to rules and policies.

Certainly, if we look at the contemporary American scene, the culture of surveillance and sanctioning is widespread, if not pervasive, in work settings. The dominant model of leadership in contemporary American management is the command-and-control approach. That model of management concentrates resources at the top of the organizational hierarchy and allows leaders to use those resources to shape employee behavior by providing incentives for desirable behavior and sanctions for undesirable behavior. This approach to leadership is sometimes referred to as "transactional leadership" because it focuses on resource-based transactions between leaders and followers. The underlying assumption is that people's behavior is a reaction to rewards and sanctions that exist in work settings.

An alternative outcome-based view is that leaders motivate employees by ensuring that they receive fair outcomes. For example, employees might feel that their rewards reflect the effort they expend to do their work ("equity"). This argument is rooted in the idea of equity theory.[8] Equity suggests that people seek fair levels of rewards from organizations and are motivated to perform when they feel that they receive them. Of course, such judgments of outcome fairness can never be completely separated from judgments about the fairness of the procedures by which the reward scheme is developed and implemented, and research indicates that people do not completely separate their judgments about distributive and procedural justice. However, distributive justice judgments are typically found to be distinct from procedural justice judgments, indicating that people view distributive and procedural justice as distinguishable.[9]

Both outcome favorability and outcome fairness models make the very reasonable assumption that people are motivated by the outcomes they receive from organizations. As a result, they argue that desirable employee behavior is motivated when people receive favorable/appropriate resources from the organization. These models suggest that, if you want rule following, you need to deliver resources.

The procedural justice literature is quite different in its focus. Although early models linked concerns with procedural justice to outcome concerns,[10] more recent models argue that people have more fundamental concerns about the fairness by which authority is exercised, concerns distinct from concerns about short-term outcome favorability or fairness. In other words, procedural justice concerns involve evaluations of the manner in which authority is exercised and decisions are made. For example, people evaluate the fairness of the procedure by which a criminal trial is conducted (such as the adversary procedure or decisions by a jury) distinctly from their judgments about whether the outcome (guilty or innocent) is accurate and the punishment fair.

Of course, the key issue is which model best describes the antecedents of employees' attitudes, values, and behaviors as they are revealed in research. Research findings are quite consistent and striking. Attitudes, values, and behaviors are strongly linked to evaluations of the procedural justice of organizational policies and practices.

Let me illustrate this finding with examples drawn from one study based on interviews with 404 employees in various organizations in the New York City area.[11] The study is designed to draw upon a wide variety of types of employees, ranging from part-time workers to highly paid executives. The interviews asked each employee about their attitudes about their work organization, their work-related values, and their work-related behaviors.

In addition, employees were asked to evaluate three aspects of the policies and practices of their organization – their distributive fairness, their favorability, and their procedural justice. In other words, employees evaluate the degree to which the policies of their work organization distribute resources fairly so that their outcomes correspond to what they deserve. They also evaluate the degree to which their outcomes are favorable – that is, high pay and benefits. Finally, they evaluate the fairness of the procedures by which their organization manages itself, such as whether the organization makes fair decisions about pay. Procedural fairness ratings included ratings of one's immediate supervisor and of the overall management of the company.

The first issue I will examine is the relationship between the policies and practices of management and indices of institutional loyalty. My concern is with the relationship between what leaders do and the institutional commitment of their employees. Institutional loyalty was measured in four ways: evaluations of one's supervisor; commitment to the organization; judgments about the morality of organizational policies; and evaluations of the legitimacy of organizational rules. Figure 7.1 shows these variables. Regression analysis was used to explore these relationships.

These results suggest that employee judgments about the fairness of the procedures used within their work setting influenced all four indices of institutional loyalty. Employees in fairly managed organizations evaluated their

Attitudes	Values	Mandatory behaviors	Voluntary behaviors
Satisfaction with leader; commitment	–	In-role behavior	Extra-role behavior
–	Legitimacy; morality	Compliance	Deference

Figure 7.1   Consequences of procedural justice

supervisor more highly, were more strongly committed to their work organization, viewed organizational policies as more consistent with their own moral values, and viewed organizational rules as more legitimate. Of these findings, it is the first two that are of particular importance. It seems reasonable that decisions made fairly would be viewed as legitimate and consistent with moral values. It is more striking that the use of procedural justice leads to positive leadership evaluations and heightened institutional commitment.

Of course, other factors also mattered. For example, supervisors were more favorably evaluated and employees were more committed when workplace policies were more favorable. Further, the rules were viewed as more legitimate when those who broke rules were punished and those who worked hard rewarded. In general, however, the primary aspect of organizational policies and practices that shaped institutional loyalty was the fairness of organizational procedures.

This examination can be extended to employee behavior, using similar regression models, but focusing on compliance/deference to rules. Compliance reflects the extent to which employees follow rules, and deference reflects employees' degree of buy-in to rules, meaning that rules are followed voluntarily, irrespective of whether detection is likely. The results support the argument that perceived procedural justice is important. Both compliance with and deference to policies are influenced by employee assessments of the fairness of workplace procedures and practices. In addition, the transactional model is also important, since people are less likely to break rules when they think it is more likely that they will be caught and punished if they do so.

However, the procedural justice effects are separate from the influences of sanctioning. These findings support the argument that perceived procedural justice is important, in this case because procedural justice shapes employee behavior.

Of course, our concern is not just about rule adherence; leaders also need to be able to motivate their members to work on behalf of the group. So, what features of the organization are associated with doing one's job and with going the extra mile? In another regression analysis, results show that organizational procedures are linked to doing one's job (in-role behavior) and engaging in voluntary behaviors (extra-role behavior).

The results for job performance illustrate the importance of engaging employees in the organization. People's in-role behavior is shaped by outcome favorability and job rewards – people do their jobs when they are materially rewarded. However, voluntary extra-role behavior is linked to the procedural justice of the workplace, as well as to job rewards. Hence, fair procedures in the workplace motivate employees to go beyond their required job tasks to do extra things that help the organization to succeed.

IMPLICATIONS FOR LEADERSHIP IN GENERAL

If leaders are to be effective in motivating those they lead, they must exercise their authority in ways that are experienced as being fair. The outlined findings, together with the large literature on procedural justice,[12] suggest that the key to motivation in organizational settings is procedural justice. I refer to this approach to leadership as process-based leadership.[13]

The root of process-based leadership is the recognition that, while leaders are generally interested in motivating followers, they are especially interested in voluntary motivation. In other words, leaders would like for their followers to buy into their vision and to believe that the goals they want to pursue are intrinsically desirable. Psychologists sometimes refer to this incorporation of the ideas and goals of the leader by followers as internalization. If followers internalize the leader's goals, then they subsequently want to achieve those goals for their own internal reasons and no longer need to be externally motivated or supervised. Employees who want their company to be successful, in other words, will work extra hours or on weekends without being asked to do so, and even without being concerned about whether their efforts will be noticed by management and rewarded. The success of the company becomes something that they value for its own sake.

To the degree that people are motivated by incentives and sanctions, the organization must continually expend resources to obtain desired behavior. Further, there are many circumstances under which it is difficult to use incentives or sanctions to motivate desirable behavior. It is often difficult to specify in advance what is desirable in a given situation, and employees are given discretion to do what they think is appropriate in a given situation. It is difficult to specify incentives or sanctions in such settings, since appropriate behavior is unclear. Even when it is clear what is desirable, it may be difficult to implement incentive and sanctioning strategies. Sanctions, in particular, require a credible surveillance system, since employees are motivated to hide rule-breaking behavior from the organization. On the other hand, if people are self-motivated, they are less influenced by incentives and sanctions.

Of course, there are two ways to activate internal motivations. One way is for the employees to internalize the values of their leader and their organization. The other way is for the organization to act in ways that are consistent with the employees' values. Either of these two approaches will result in voluntary deference to leaders. However, the ability of leaders to encourage the internalization of values leads to much greater freedom of action for leaders, since activating employees' own moral values requires that leaders act in ways that are consistent with those values.

This same distinction is reflected in the difference between legitimacy and moral consistency. If leaders are legitimate, they are authorized to determine the appropriate course of action within some domain within which they have legitimacy. Within that arena, followers should defer to the decisions of their legitimate leader. However, moral consistency requires that the actions taken be in accord with the values of the followers involved. Hence, legitimacy grants leaders greater freedom of action. Conversely, it is harder to internalize values in followers in order to gain legitimacy than it is to appeal to values that they already possess. In both cases, however, the gain for the leader is that followers follow them willingly.

THE LEADER BEHAVIORS THAT SHAPE PROCEDURAL FAIRNESS JUDGMENTS

To address the more specific leadership implications of these findings, we need to examine what people mean by procedural fairness. Studies typically find seven, eight, or even more procedural elements that contribute to assessments of their procedural fairness.[14] However, two elements of procedures are the primary factors that contribute to judgments about their fairness: the quality of decision making (that is, the neutrality of the procedure) and the quality of interpersonal treatment (that is, the degree to which people receive treatment with dignity and respect and the trustworthiness of the leader).

The Quality of Decision Making

Neutrality

Neutral rules are rules that create a "level playing field" in which no one is unfairly disadvantaged and no one is unfairly privileged. In other words, rules themselves can be neutral or biased. So, for example, employees might expect that their pay would be based upon the quality and quantity of their work, rather than upon their religion or gender, their friendship with their boss, or their personal lifestyle. A rule that linked pay to merit would be neutral, in that it would indicate that work-related criteria should be used in decision making, and that other criteria should not.

The neutrality of a procedure is also manifested by evidence that the authorities implementing the rules are impartial and do not favor one party over another for reasons of personal opinion, personal bias, or personal prejudice. Neutrality is reflected in decision making that is objective in the sense that the decision makers base their decisions on evidence about the facts involved and that they apply rules consistently across people and situations.

If employees believe that the authorities are following such neutral or impartial rules and making factual, objective, decisions, they think procedures are fairer. Of course, it is important to recognize that these ideas flow from the subjective study of fairness and reflect the attributes of procedures that people associate with saying that the procedures are fair.

Neutrality directly addresses the issue of identity security. When people have their identity intertwined with an organization, they are vulnerable to having that identity demeaned or damaged when they receive negative feedback from the group about their status. If people know that the procedures of the group are factual and unbiased, they know the decisions will not reflect personal prejudices and will be based on the consistent application of rules to all parties.

Neutrality is especially important to people who are in groups that have the potential to be stigmatized, that is, women and minorities. These groups could be the target of stereotyping and prejudice, so they are especially concerned about evidence that their identities will be protected by the use of fair procedures within the organizations to which they belong.

Finally, it is important to note that neutrality, as discussed here, is a procedural characteristic. It would be anticipated that using a neutral procedure would lead to a fair outcome, and studies typically find that judgments about procedural justice and distributive justice are correlated within a given situation. However, those same studies find that people do not simply equate procedural and distributive fairness. Procedural fairness is linked to distinct procedural attributes of consistency, factuality, and lack of bias. People are able to evaluate the fairness of procedures without knowing their outcomes.

The Quality of Interpersonal Treatment

Treatment with dignity and respect

Studies show that people value the respect that others show for their rights and their status within society. They are very concerned that, in the process of dealing with authorities, their dignity as people and as members of society is recognized and acknowledged. This involves respect for them as persons and for their rights as members of the organization.

Studies consistently find that people in vulnerable groups – women and minorities, for example – focus on whether or not they receive respect when dealing with authorities. Because the members of these groups are potentially subject to exclusion and to demeaning behavior, they are attentive to signs that their status in the group is low.[15]

The importance which people place upon an affirmation of their status is especially relevant to leadership, given that politeness and respect are essentially unrelated to the outcomes people receive when they deal with social authorities. More than any other issue, treatment with dignity and respect is something that authorities can give to everyone with whom they deal.

The trustworthiness of the authorities

Another factor shaping people's views about the fairness of a procedure is their assessment of the motives or intentions of the third-party authority responsible for resolving the case. People recognize that third parties typically have considerable discretion to implement formal procedures in varying ways, and they are concerned about the motivation underlying the decisions made by the authority with which they are dealing. They make judgments about whether that person is benevolent and caring, is concerned about their situation and needs, considers their arguments, tries to do what is right for them, and tries to be fair. All of these elements combine to shape a general assessment of the person's trustworthiness.

Interestingly, judgments about the trustworthiness of the authorities are the primary factors shaping evaluations of the fairness of the procedures used by those authorities.[16] People recognize that their leaders could potentially use their positions of leadership to enact self-serving policies at the expense of their subordinates. Leaders are exercising fiduciary trust, and followers focus on whether they believe that leaders are, in fact, acting on behalf of their agents (that is, their followers).

The importance of trust is illustrated by a finding of the literature on participation. People value the opportunity to speak to authorities only if they believe that the authority is sincerely considering their arguments. When they trust that the authority sincerely considered their arguments, even if the arguments were then rejected, this leads to the evaluation of procedures as fairer.

I have already outlined the importance of neutrality to assessments of the fairness of procedures. There is considerable evidence that the basis of the authoritativeness – the ability of authorities to gain deference to their decisions – is shifting from a neutrality base to a trust base. That is, in the past authorities have often gained their authoritativeness through the neutral application of rules, that is, through the use of formal decision-making procedures that are objective and factual in character.

A person, for example, can go to any police officer or judge and receive more or less equivalent treatment and outcomes, since the particular authority with whom they are dealing will be following universal rules. Having personal knowledge about the specific authority involved in an interaction is not important. On the other hand, trust is linked to judgments about particular authorities and, hence, to particularized, personal connections between citizens and authorities. For example, people might get to know a beat cop because that person patrols their neighborhood. They have dealt with him and know his motives and values. Consequently, they feel that they can trust him.

An organization can gain deference by having formal rules that reflect neutrality. It can also gain deference through the personal relationships that exist between employees and their own particular supervisors. The former approach reflects a neutrality model of procedural fairness, the latter approach a trust-based model. Similarly, the police can gain deference when they are viewed as following professional rules of conduct and uniform, unbiased procedures; particular police officers can be respected and known in their communities and can gain deference through their personalized connections.

AN EMPIRICAL ASSESSMENT

The conceptual framework outlined for understanding these various aspects of procedural justice is shown in Figure 7.2. Using the employee sample I have already described, we can examine the importance of the different factors outlined as elements of overall procedural justice. To do so, we use regression analysis to explore the degree to which overall judgments about the fairness or unfairness of organizational procedures are linked to assessments of the fairness of various components of the organization.

What Influences Procedural Justice Judgments?

While we have focused upon two key elements of procedural justice – decision making and interpersonal treatment – it is important to explore how people determine their fairness. In particular, two aspects of organizations are

	Procedural justice elements	Relational issues
Quality of decision making	Neutrality	Rule-based; factual; consistent; unbiased
Quality of interpersonal treatment	– Status recognition – Trustworthiness	Respect for person; for rights Concern for welfare
Outcomes	– Outcome fairness – Outcome valuence	– Policy favorability – Behavior linked to incentives/sanctions – Total job rewards

Figure 7.2   Components of procedural justice

often associated with procedural fairness: whether there are opportunities for participation and whether management accounts for or explains its actions.

Participation

Procedural justice theorists argue that people feel more fairly treated if they are allowed to participate in the resolution of their problems or conflicts by presenting their suggestions about what should be done. Such opportunities are referred to as *process control* or *voice*. The positive effects of participation were first documented in the work of Thibaut and Walker[17] and have been subsequently documented in numerous other studies on topics such as plea bargaining,[18] sentencing hearings,[19] and mediation.[20] In all of these diverse settings, people feel more fairly treated when they are given an opportunity to make arguments about what should be done to resolve a problem or conflict.

Participation effects have been found to be enhanced when people feel that the things they say are shaping the outcomes of the dispute, that is, when they have an instrumental influence.[21] However, voice effects have not been found to be dependent just upon having control over the actual outcomes of conflicts. People have also been found to value the opportunity to express their views to decision makers in situations in which they believe that what they are saying has little or no influence upon the decisions being made.[22] For example, victims value the opportunity to speak at sentencing hearings irrespective of whether their arguments influence the sentences given to the criminals involved.[23]

The findings about the importance of process control or voice suggest that people are interested in both sharing the discussion over the issues involved in their problem or conflict and controlling decisions about how to handle it. In fact, people often look to societal authorities to make decisions about which legal or managerial principles ought to govern the resolution of their dispute. In other words, they expect societal authorities to make final decisions about how to act based upon what they have said.

The finding that people value the opportunity to participate by expressing their opinions and stating their case helps to explain why people like mediation. Mediation is typically rated as providing greater opportunities for participation than formal trials.[24] Similarly, defendants involved in disposing of felony charges against themselves indicate that they have greater opportunities to participate in plea bargaining than in a formal trial,[25] and they rate plea bargaining to be a fairer procedure for resolving their case.

When we include measures of participation in the regression equation, we do not find that participation independently shapes procedural justice ratings. This is consistent with the finding of Lind, Tyler, and Huo.[26] But we do find that participation has an indirect role. Specifically, process-control judgments are important in shaping people's assessments of interpersonal treatment. Employees judge procedures that do not include voice or process control to be disrespectful.

Accountability

How can authorities communicate that they are trying to be fair? A key antecedent is justification. When authorities are presenting their decisions to the people influenced by them, they need to make clear that they have listened to and considered the arguments made. They can do so by accounting for their decisions. Such accounts should clearly state the arguments made by the various parties to the dispute. They should also explain how those arguments have been considered and why they have been accepted or rejected.

Regression analysis indicates that accounting for decisions is strongly associated with both fair decision making and with respectful treatment. Hence, when authorities explain clearly and honestly why they have made their decisions, they increase the perceived fairness of the decision-making procedure. They also lead people to feel more highly respected and valued. Another way to put this is that accountability leads people to feel respected and to trust the authorities with whom they are dealing.

Implications

These findings suggest that there are two key issues that shape procedural fairness. The first involves the neutrality and impartiality in the creation and application of rules; the use of facts, not biases, when making implementation decisions; consistency of application across people and situations. All of these issues refer to the arena of decision making and are linked to traditional models of the exercise of authority.[27]

In addition, people are clearly influenced by their judgments about the quality of the interpersonal treatment they experience when dealing with others. This concern reflects both a desire for polite and respectful treatment and a sensitivity to the rights associated with both being a person and being a member of a group. This interpersonal aspect of procedural fairness is consistently found to be as important as is the more traditionally studied question of decision making.

Levels of Leadership: The Four-Component Model of Procedural Justice

Leadership potentially involves dealing with both the immediate supervisor with whom an employee has direct personal contact and the larger organizational framework and leadership structure. In a large company, for example, many employees may never have met their company's top leaders, who are part of a large institutional framework. They will, however, have a personal relationship with their immediate supervisor. This distinction is built into the four-component model, shown in Figure 7.3, which suggests that both levels are important.[28]

We can test this importance in our sample of employees. When we do so, we find that all four factors – supervisory procedural fairness and interpersonal

	Supervisor	Organization
Quality of decision-making	Neutrality in decision-making; lack of personal bias	Factual, objective standards, consistently applied
Quality of interpersonal treatment	Polite; respectful	Acknowledge rights and needs of employees
Outcomes	Valence of decisions	Valence of policies and practices

Figure 7.3   The four component model of procedural justice

treatment, and organizational procedural fairness and interpersonal treatment – are important. The implication of this finding is that leadership must be concerned both with particular personal relationships that involve leadership in small groups and with the broader leadership of organizational authorities. Both influence people in work settings.

SUMMARY

There are lots of reasons for leaders to act ethically in organizational settings. One is their responsibility to their own moral principles and/or to the professional norms that govern the conduct of leaders.[29] Such norms are often enshrined in codes of conduct for accountants, doctors, lawyers, judges, and so on. They prescribe the appropriate behaviors linked to the obligations and responsibilities of leadership roles. There are normative reasons for ethical behavior that are well specified in the many discussions of the philosophical basis of ethics found in other chapters in this volume.

My approach points to a different reason for supporting ethical conduct by people in positions of leadership: the perception of the leader's fairness has a strong influence on the behavior of followers. In my view, this psychological approach to ethics is highly congruent with the philosophical approach. The philosophical approach indicates that people should care about ethics, while the behavioral approach indicates that the people in organizations do care about experiencing an ethical climate within the organization to which they belong.

The findings outlined are consistent with the general suggestion that fair decision-making procedures encourage voluntary cooperation with groups because they lead to identification with and loyalty and commitment to groups.[30]

Similarly, procedural justice promotes deference to social rules because it promotes the belief that organizational policies are moral and organizational authorities are legitimate. These internal values are important because when people feel that rules are moral and authorities ought to be obeyed, they take responsibility and voluntarily defer to the rules and authorities.

In both of these cases, procedural justice is central to creating and maintaining internal attitudes and values that support voluntary cooperative behavior on the part of the members of groups. The importance of developing and maintaining such attitudes and values is increasingly being emphasized, as social scientists recognize the limits of leadership strategies that seek to shape the rewards and punishments received by the parties to a dispute.

Recent social science thinking has been dominated by rational choice models of the person. As a consequence, command-and-control, deterrence, or social control strategies have dominated discussions about management and regulation. These strategies focus upon the individual as a calculative actor, thinking, feeling, and behaving in terms of potential rewards and costs in their immediate environment.

Increasingly, social scientists have recognized the limits of command-and-control approaches to managing. In political and legal settings, authorities have recognized that both regulation[31] and the encouragement of voluntary civic behavior[32] are difficult when authorities can rely only upon their ability to reward and/or punish citizens. Similarly, organizational theorists are recognizing the difficulties of managing employees using command-and-control strategies.[33]

The alternative to such strategies is to focus on approaches based upon appeals to internal attitudes and values. If people have internal attitudes and values that lead them to act voluntarily in pro-social ways that help the group, including extra-role behavior and deference to authority, then authorities need not seek to compel such behavior through promises of reward or threats of punishment. They can rely instead upon people's willingness to engage in the behavior voluntarily.

Research such as that considered here suggests that using fair decision-making procedures is central to the development and maintenance of supportive internal values. People view authorities who use fair decision-making procedures more positively, specifically, as more moral and legitimate. These perceptions of morality and legitimacy make them more willing to defer to the authorities' policies, rules, and organizational decisions. This produces uniformity of behavior in line with organizational rules and the decisions of organizational authorities.

Organizations that use fair decision-making procedures also encourage commitment and identification on the part of their members, which leads to voluntary cooperative behavior. People want the group to succeed and engage in behaviors to help achieve that objective. In other words, people willingly engage their own creative efforts and energies in efforts to advance the interests of the group. They might help others do their jobs during a crisis; help and encourage new group members; or engage in activities which are unobservable and, hence, will not be rewarded, but which help the group. Authorities can appeal to their legitimacy as leaders when they want people to cooperate.

In other words, the recognition of the importance of creating a "civic culture" or an "organizational culture" which supports the development and maintenance of internal attitudes and values among group members is increasing as the limits of command-and-control approaches to managing conflict become clearer. Procedural justice is central to both developing and maintaining judgments that authorities are legitimate and feelings of commitment and identification with groups, organizations, and societies.

In addition, the approach outlined illustrates the value of an empirical approach to studying both leadership and ethics. Philosophical treatments of ethics examine the ethical criteria that ought to govern decisions made by people in positions of authority within work organizations.[34] Empirical research gives force to this philosophical analysis by showing that people are motivated by ethical concerns that go beyond their self-interest. Empirical studies further suggest that the key ethical issues identified by philosophers fit closely with the intuitions about justice and morality that emerge from interviews with the members of organizations. While everyday employees are not moral philosophers, it is noteworthy that they recognize many of the issues that dominate the discussions of moral philosophers. Hence, empirical research reveals the richness of the ethical thinking of everyday people. In both of these ways this empirical approach converges strikingly with the intuitions of ethical theorists.

NOTES

1. "Is Your Boss a Crook?" *CNNmoney* (January 16, 2004). Retrieved December 17, 2004, from http://money.cnn.com/2004/01/15/pf/boss_ethical/index.htm
2. Ethics Resource Center, *2000 National Business Ethics Survey* (2000). Retrieved December 20, 2004, from http://www.ethics.org/2000survey.html; Ethics Resource Center, *2003 National Business Ethics Survey*[SM] (May 21, 2003). Retrieved December 20, 2004, from http://www.ethics.org/nbes2003/index.html
3. "Is Your Boss a Crook?" *CNNmoney*.
4. Leslie Haggin Geary, "I Quit! Overworked Employees Are Fed Up: A Survey Finds 8 Out of 10 Americans Want a New Job," *CNNmoney* (December 30, 2003). Retrieved December 17, 2004, from http://money.cnn.com/2003/11/11/pf/q_iquit/index.htm?cnn=yes
5. Robert Levering, *A Great Place to Work: What Makes Some Employers So Good, and Most So Bad* (New York: Random House, 1988); Charles A. O'Reilly and Jeffrey Pfeffer, *Hidden Value: How Great Companies Achieve Extraordinary Results with Ordinary People* (Boston, MA: Harvard Business School Press, 2000); Robert C. Solomon, *Ethics and Excellence: Cooperation and Integrity in Business* (New York: Oxford University Press, 1992).
6. Jerald Greenberg, "Equity and Workplace Status: A Field Experiment," *Journal of Applied Psychology* 73 (1988): 606–13; Robert D. Pritchard, Marvin D. Dunnette and Dale O. Jorgenson, "Effects of Perceptions of Equity and Inequity on Worker Performance and Satisfaction," *Journal of Applied Psychology* 56 (1972): 75–94; David R. Schmitt and Gerald Marwell, "Withdrawal and Reward Reallocation as Responses to Inequity," *Journal of Experimental Social Psychology* 8 (1972): 207–21.
7. Tom R. Tyler, "Justice, Identity and Leadership," in Daan van Knippenberg and Michael A. Hogg (eds), *Leadership and Power: Identity Processes in Groups and Organizations* (Thousand Oaks, CA: Sage, 2003), pp. 94–108; Tom R. Tyler, "Process-Based Leadership: How Do Leaders Lead?" in David M. Messick and Roderick M. Kramer (eds), *The Psychology of Leadership: New Perspectives and Research* (Mahwah, NJ: Erlbaum, 2005), pp. 163–89.
8. Tom R. Tyler, Robert J. Boeckmann, Heather J. Smith and Yuen J. Huo, *Social Justice in a Diverse Society* (Boulder, CO: Westview, 1997).
9. Tom R. Tyler and Heather J. Smith, "Social Justice and Social Movements," in Daniel T. Gilbert, Susan T. Fiske, and Gardner Lindzey (eds), *Handbook of Social Psychology*, 4th edn, Vol. 2 (Boston, MA: McGraw-Hill, 1998), pp. 595–629.

10. John Thibaut and Laurens Walker, *Procedural Justice: A Psychological Analysis* (Hillsdale, NJ: Erlbaum, 1975).
11. Tom R. Tyler and Steven L. Blader, *Cooperation in Groups: Procedural Justice, Social Identity, and Behavioral Engagement* (Philadelphia, PA: Psychology Press, 2000).
12. E. Allan Lind and Tom R. Tyler, *The Social Psychology of Procedural Justice* (New York: Plenum, 1988); Tom R. Tyler and E. Allan Lind, "A Relational Model of Authority in Groups," in Mark P. Zanna (ed.), *Advances in Experimental Social Psychology*, Vol. 25 (San Diego, CA: Academic Press, 1992), pp. 115–91.
13. Tyler, "Justice, Identity and Leadership"; Tyler, "Process-Based Leadership."
14. Robin I. Lissak and Blair H. Sheppard, "Beyond Fairness: The Criterion Problem in Research on Dispute Intervention," *Journal of Applied Social Psychology* 13 (1983): 45–65; Blair H. Sheppard and Roy J. Lewicki, "Toward General Principles of Managerial Fairness," *Social Justice Research* 1 (1987): 161–76; Tom R. Tyler, "What Is Procedural Justice? Criteria Used by Citizens to Assess the Fairness of Legal Procedures," *Law and Society Review* 22 (1988): 103–35.
15. Tom R. Tyler and Yuen J. Huo, *Trust in the Law: Encouraging Public Cooperation with the Police and Courts* (New York: Russell Sage Foundation, 2002).
16. Tyler and Lind, "A Relational Model of Authority in Groups."
17. Thibaut and Walker, *Procedural Justice.*
18. Pauline Houlden, "Impact of Procedural Modifications on Evaluations of Plea Bargaining," *Law and Society Review* 15 (1980–81): 267–91.
19. Anne M. Heinz and Wayne A. Kerstetter, "Pretrial Settlement Conference: Evaluation of a Reform in Plea Bargaining," *Law and Society Review* 13 (1979): 349–66.
20. Katherine M. Kitzmann and Robert E. Emery, "Procedural Justice and Parents' Satisfaction in a Field Study of Child Custody Dispute Resolution," *Law and Human Behavior* 17 (1993): 553–67; Robert J. MacCoun, E. Allan Lind, Deborah R. Hensler, David L. Bryant and Patricia A. Ebener, *Alternative Adjudication: An Evaluation of the New Jersey Automobile Arbitration Program* (Santa Monica, CA: Rand, 1988); Debra L. Shapiro and Jeanne M. Brett, "Comparing Three Processes Underlying Judgments of Procedural Justice: A Field Study of Mediation and Arbitration," *Journal of Personality and Social Psychology* 65 (1993): 1167–77.
21. Shapiro and Brett, "Comparing Three Processes Underlying Judgments of Procedural Justice."
22. E. Allan Lind, Ruth Kanfer and P. Christopher Earley, "Voice, Control, and Procedural Justice: Instrumental and Noninstrumental Concerns in Fairness Judgments," *Journal of Personality and Social Psychology* 59 (1990): 952–9; Tom R. Tyler, "Conditions Leading to Value-Expressive Effects in Judgments of Procedural Justice: A Test of Four Models," *Journal of Personality and Social Psychology* 52 (1987): 333–44.
23. Heinz and Kerstetter, "Pretrial Settlement Conference."
24. Craig A. McEwen and Richard J. Maiman, "Mediation in Small Claims Court: Achieving Compliance through Consent," *Law and Society Review* 18 (1984): 11–49.
25. Jonathan D. Casper, Tom R. Tyler and Bonnie Fisher, "Procedural Justice in Felony Cases," *Law and Society Review* 22 (1988): 483–507.
26. E. Allan Lind, Tom R. Tyler and Yuen J. Huo, "Procedural Context and Culture: Variation in the Antecedents of Procedural Justice Judgments," *Journal of Personality and Social Psychology* 73 (1997): 767–80.
27. Thibaut and Walker, *Procedural Justice.*
28. Steven L. Blader and Tom R. Tyler, "A Four-Component Model of Procedural Justice: Defining the Meaning of a 'Fair' Process," *Personality and Social Psychology Bulletin* 29 (2003): 747–58.
29. Norman E. Bowie, *Business Ethics: A Kantian Perspective* (Malden, MA: Blackwell, 1999).
30. Robert Folger and Mary A. Konovsky, "Effects of Procedural and Distributive Justice on Reactions to Pay Raise Decisions," *Academy of Management Journal* 32 (1989): 115–30; M. Audrey Korsgaard, David M. Schweiger and Harry J. Sapienza, "Building Commitment, Attachment, and Trust in Strategic Decision-Making Teams: The Role of Procedural Justice," *Academy of Management Journal* 38 (1995): 60–84; Dean B. McFarlin and Paul

D. Sweeney, "Distributive and Procedural Justice as Predictors of Satisfaction with Personal and Organizational Outcomes," *Academy of Management Journal* 35 (1992): 626–37; John Schaubroeck, Douglas R. May and F. William Brown, "Procedural Justice Explanations and Employee Reactions to Economic Hardship: A Field Experiment," *Journal of Applied Psychology* 79 (1994): 455–60; M. Susan Taylor, Kay B. Tracy, Monika K. Renard, J. Kline Harrison and Stephen J. Carroll, "Due Process in Performance Appraisal: A Quasi-Experiment in Procedural Justice," *Administrative Science Quarterly* 40 (1995): 495–523.

31. Tom R. Tyler, *Why People Obey the Law* (New Haven, CT: Yale University Press, 1990); Tom R. Tyler, "Trust and Law Abidingness: A Proactive Model of Social Regulation," *Boston University Law Review* 81 (2001): 361–406.

32. Donald P. Green and Ian Shapiro, *Pathologies of Rational Choice Theory: A Critique of Applications in Political Science* (New Haven, CT: Yale University Press, 1994).

33. Jeffrey Pfeffer, *Competitive Advantage through People: Unleashing the Power of the Work Force* (Boston, MA: Harvard Business School Press, 1994).

34. Bowie, *Business Ethics*; Marshall Schminke, *Managerial Ethics: Moral Management of People and Processes* (Mahwah, NJ: Erlbaum, 1998).

8. That which governs best: leadership, ethics and human systems

S.D. Noam Cook

In an important sense, the better leadership is at doing its job, the less need there is for leaders to make interventions in the workings of the governed. Much of what a good leader does, accordingly, is not a matter of dealing dramatically with overt challenges, but of establishing and maintaining a smoothly functioning system. This role may not be as glamorous as those more commonly associated with good leaders, but I believe it is leadership's prime responsibility, especially when it comes to ethics. Knowing when to intervene and when not to is a critical skill for all leaders. An accomplished ship's captain knows when to keep a light hand on the rudder.[1] This point is captured in the opening passage in Henry David Thoreau's 1848 Essay "Civil Disobedience,"[2] to which the title of this chapter alludes: "I heartily accept the motto, 'That government is best which governs least'; and I should like to see it acted up to more rapidly and systematically."

This is of one the most familiar quotes from Thoreau, and one of the most broadly misunderstood. In recent years, it has been routinely misunderstood (or misused) by advocates for smaller government and lower taxes. Noting this misunderstanding helps clarify the value of Thoreau's point for the subject at hand. The size of the government and the level of taxation are solely instrumental; they are the means by which government carries out its functions. In a democracy, the people should decide what the functions of the government are, and the size of government and the level of taxation should be set in proportion to those functions. (Just as the size and costs of administration in any kind of social system should be no more and no less than what is necessary to carry out the mandates of its stakeholders.) To claim that government should be smaller and taxes lower without identifying specific functions calling for that size and level sidesteps discussion of what the people want the government to do, and is therefore anti-democratic.

Diminishing the means of democracy (either as an end in itself or at the service of ends outside of governance) is not what Thoreau had in mind. Indeed, Thoreau's views are quite different, far more democratic, and for our purposes much more powerful. He is saying, first of all, that leaders need to know when their direct involvement is called for and when it is not. That is, a good leader must be able to shift from intervention to stewardship.

LEADERSHIP AS STEWARDSHIP

This point is made delightfully clear in an example drawn from orchestral conducting (since I sing with a symphony chorus, conductors have become one of my favorite sources of insight concerning leadership). As a young man in the early 1950s, André Previn studied with the renowned conductor Pierre Monteux, then music director of the San Francisco Symphony. A few years later, Monteux attended a concert Previn conducted with another orchestra. Backstage after the concert, Previn was eager to hear what his teacher thought of the performance. Monteux paid Previn some initial complements, then said, "In the last movement of the Haydn Symphony, my dear, did you think the orchestra was playing well?" Previn nervously reviewed the movement in his head, and "fearing the worst" finally said he thought "the orchestra had indeed played very well." Monteux smiled and said, "So do I. Next time, don't interfere."[3]

The lesson in this is not that there are times when a leader should do nothing. Rather, it is that when one's organization is functioning well, the responsibility of leadership is to help maintain that state, not redirect it. A leader, meanwhile, may have a great deal of work to do in helping an organization get to the point where this is possible.

The next passage in Thoreau's essay helps further this notion. "Carried out," he writes, "it finally amounts to this, which I also believe 'that government is best which governs not at all'; and when men are prepared for it, that is the kind of government that they will have."

Although idealistic in tone, there is an implication to this passage that is utterly practical. The phrase "when men are prepared for it" points to the fact that what makes it possible for leadership to "govern less" (to say nothing of "not at all") is the extent to which the governed possess a sound constitution – that is, that the orchestra has been properly rehearsed, the team fully trained, the organization appropriately designed, the community well organized. It is only when the course is properly set, the crew well disciplined, and the ship in good order that the accomplished ship's captain can keep a light hand on the rudder. When the members of any human group are "prepared for it," the leadership role can and should shift from intervention to stewardship.

This is especially true when it comes to ethics. It is probably the case more often than we would like to believe that exemplary moral intervention by leadership is actually a sign that leadership did not do its job in the first place. If the governed have been "prepared for it," if they have been encouraged to treat consideration of ethics as part of normal operations and have been given the tools for doing so, the need for moral crisis intervention by leaders ought to be diminished.

LEADERSHIP AND SYSTEMS

Just as good leadership – especially good ethical leadership – requires knowing when to intervene and when to provide stewardship, it also requires knowing what kind of thing one is leading and how ethics is a part of it. To govern best I believe one needs to recognize that the people in one's charge are not a random collection of individuals, but people whose coordinated actions form them into a system. In fact, one of the fundamental responsibilities of a leader is to help groups of individuals act systematically. Our understanding of the place of ethics within a system and the role of leadership with respect to it, therefore, can be influenced by what we understand a system to be and how differences among kinds of systems can influence the way we address ethical issues. So it is necessary to have an understanding of systems that will enable us to see ethics and leadership from a systems perspective.

There is now a well-established history of understanding human groups as systems. A classic foundation for this can be found in such areas as the early work on cybernetics[4] and general systems theory.[5] Since the 1960s at least, organizational theorists have developed various models for seeing organizations as systems for coordinating the work of people and machines, allocating tasks, making decisions, and so on.[6] In a broader sense, a systems perspective has also been applied to the adaptive character of human groups and the human mind in general.[7]

A general theme within this work has been to see computational devices, the environment, human groups, and so on, as sharing certain characteristics that can be validly and usefully understood as systemic. Within this perspective, Sir Geoffrey Vickers argued that just as it is important to see all of these as systems, it is equally important to see them as different kinds of systems.[8] It was Sir Geoffrey's contention that there are at least three distinct kinds of systems, which he identified as natural, man-made and human (akin, in my view, to Arendt's distinctions among labor, work and action[9]). And Vickers held that each is unique with respect to its requirements for sustenance and stability. This view also calls for an understanding of the place of ethics with respect to different kinds of systems.

THREE KINDS OF SYSTEMS

In his essay of 1893, "Evolution and Ethics," T.H. Huxley draws a now-classic distinction between a jungle and a garden.[10] A jungle can be explained in terms of the push and pull of evolutionary adaptation, the vagaries of weather, and other such workings of nature. These days, we can easily point to jungles along with other ecological niches as exemplars of what we can call "natural systems." We have become increasingly more sophisticated at specifying the characteristics of natural systems, particularly as they operate under the impact of human activity (reflecting the distinction, as Dewey notes, between our "living in" and "living by means of" the environment[11]).

The same natural forces that we find in a jungle are equally at work in a garden. In fact, if we fail to look after a garden's basic needs as part of the plant kingdom, it will fade or die. Unlike a jungle, however, a garden cannot be explained solely by appeal to the workings of nature. Gardens are artifacts. They are human creations, jungles upon which design of uniquely human origin has been imposed. If we fail to look after a garden's design, it will revert all too quickly to the state of nature from which it was drawn. Accordingly, any satisfactory explanation of the form and function of a garden requires appeal to both the requirements of nature and to the human purposes of its design.

This is true, building on Vickers, of all such systems. Whether gardens or cities, tools or technologies, automobiles or the Internet, they are all a mixture of natural elements and design, and both aspects demand our attention. A bridge must be explained equally in terms of the functions its design affords, and the properties of its raw materials that afford that design.[12] Because such systems are artifacts, and because their forum and functions are not adequately explained in terms of properties of natural systems, I wish to call them "artifactual" systems. (I prefer this term to "man-made" since it is gender-neutral, and to "artificial" because that can suggest "phony," which artifactual systems clearly are not. "Artifactual" is meant to remind us that such systems are human creations.)

As human beings, we interact not only with nature and with our artifacts but also with other people. That aspect of our interactions with one another that is distinct from the mediation of either nature or artifacts is what can be understood as the workings of "human systems." These systems include all forms of human interaction, from dialogue to teamwork to organizational behavior to the modes of discourse necessary to vital public life.

Human systems also entail those standards that give form and direction to human activity – particularly, our aesthetic and moral values. The actions we take and the choices we make reflect our values. They can also be seen in what we do with respect to all three kinds of systems. How we shape or despoil nature, what artifacts we choose to create and how we use them, and the ways we treat one another all testify to what our values are. In explaining the form a garden takes, for example, we need to refer to those things of human origin that have been incorporated into the garden's design: the aesthetic traditions that enable us to distinguish an English garden from a Japanese one, and by which we judge one garden to be modest and another world-class.

All three kinds of systems also interact with one another, and the flourishing of one can depend on the stability of the others. Just as we can see the artifactual system of a garden fail when we ignore its needs as a natural system, so can we see technologies fail when we ignore the requirements of the human systems within which they must function. Likewise, the fact that a garden will revert all too quickly to jungle if its needs as an artifactual system are not met has parallels in the case of cities, organizations and technologies – each one of which has its own version of reverting to jungle.

If our systems are to function well ethically and not just technically, then ethics needs to be one of the "controls" or "regulators" that we draw on to decide what is a desirable configuration of a system and an acceptable direction to go with it.[13] Leaders have a powerful hand on these controls, and the form and course a system takes can reflect what leaders do, or fail to do, with them. Ideally, we seek moral smooth sailing. But at times, instability and ethical problems can be a result of a failure to take the controls, or of oversteering or understeering the system.

WHEN LEADERS FAIL TO STEER THE SYSTEM: THE MYTH OF "BAD APPLES"

Although it is common to hear talk about systems, the systemic level is sometimes ignored in public and business life, particularly if the subject is ethics. When unethical behavior makes the news, it is not surprising to hear leaders refer to "a few bad apples" before or instead of talking about systemic failure. In fact, corporate, political and military leaders have even been known to brush aside suggestions that there might be a systemic component to such cases. Recently in the US, for example, "bad apples" is literally how leaders from the White House to Congress to corporate boardrooms repeatedly characterized the issue of the mistreatment of prisoners held by US forces in Iraq, and the Enron, Arthur Andersen and WorldCom scandals. In some instances, an initial bad apple approach has been followed by a legislative hearing, commission or investigation charged with assessing systemic problems, as we have seen in the US in such high profile cases as the studies of NASA project failures, the 9/11 commission and the evaluation of intelligence services. Still, when leaders, particularly initially, characterize ethically questionable situations in terms of bad apples (perhaps as an attempt to get themselves off the hook) they may be missing an opportunity to take charge and set the tone of efforts to assess what ethical problems there may in fact be in the systems they lead.

Once leaders set the focus on the level of individuals, the bad apples theory can frustrate efforts to diagnose problems and to create remedies at the systemic level. In the context of recent legislative and commission investigations into systemic failures, for example, many political leaders have publicly called only for stricter laws and harsher punishments, which themselves tend to focus on curbing the behavior of individuals. Moves of this sort can actually serve (deliberately or not) as a means to avoid changing a system.

There are some things that we do as groups that we cannot do as well or at all as individuals, such as play basketball, perform symphonies, fight fires, do leading edge industrial research, implement national policies, provide goods and services to a global market, and so on. This is a central reason why we create teams, governments, corporations and the like, and set up ways for making collective decisions and taking collective action through them.[14] We design them to function as they do. And since these functions can have a positive or negative impact on the wellbeing of people, animals and the environment, they are open to moral evaluation. That is, the activities of groups are in large measure a product of how they are designed to function as systems, and because there is a systemic component to their functions, there needs to be a systemic level to any moral assessment of those functions. Whether personally or through commissions, panels, committees and the like, the power of leadership can guide assessments of the possibility that something about the design of the systems they oversee may permit or even encourage unethical behavior.

WHEN LEADERS OVERSTEER THE SYSTEM: SQUELCHING PUBLIC DISCUSSION OF ETHICS

Every human system has a technological infrastructure for public discussion. It can be a town square, a board meeting, a water cooler, a secret code or whatever provides the means for public communication within a given group. Whether the flow of public discussion is flourishing or curbed, the infrastructure exists: it is part of what it means for a group of individuals to be integrated into a system. If ethics is to be dealt with in a proactive and practical manner, leaders need to assure that there are appropriate infrastructures in place that afford public discussion of ethics.

I was once a member of an email list that went out to everyone working in a corporate division housed in a single building. The email list was used for announcements and exchanges relevant to people in that division. One morning a message appeared from an ad hoc group in the building concerning the division's annual contribution to the United Way. The message encouraged people to contribute, but asked them to attach to their donation a request that United Way not use any of the money to support the Boy Scouts of America because it discriminates on the basis of sexual orientation. A few minutes later a second email appeared saying "Hey, don't pick on the Boy Scouts. It's a great organization." This was quickly followed by a message from a person in the ad hoc group to the effect that "We agree. It is a great organization. That's why we think gay people should not be excluded." After that, I watched with delight as a rather articulate and serious discussion slowly developed on the email list. The topic was clearly of concern to people, and since within the culture of that division the email list functioned as a kind of high-tech town square, it seemed to me the obvious place for this discussion to occur. Nonetheless, a couple of hours into the discussion, a senior manager added a message that read essentially, "Don't debate this here. If you agree with the ad hoc group, act accordingly. If you agree with the others, follow them."

With that, the discussion ended. There was not a single further posting. This was very disappointing to me because it seemed that a productive discussion of an ethical issue had been taking place through an appropriate and efficient infrastructure for it. The email list provided a means for publicly addressing an ethical issue of common concern. The senior manager ended the ethical debate by exercising a leadership role the way he did. In essence, the system was functioning effectively (like André Previn's orchestra in the example above, the group was "playing well"). The manager brought the system to a halt by asserting an interventionist leadership role (rather than simply maintaining oversight) in an otherwise leaderless group.

I later asked him why he had stopped the discussion. He indicated that he felt the list was "not the right place" for it, and that "if people want to debate it they can set up a special email list for that purpose and not bother everyone with a controversial topic."

This seemed to me to miss a number of things that are crucial to dealing effectively with ethical issues. All ethical issues are potentially controversial. That is one reason why they call for public discussion. In this group, issues affecting the division were often dealt with through the list. So the list was a good place for this discussion to occur. Also, the "special email list" he suggested would not *enable* public discussion; it would *squelch* it. True public discussion requires that differing views come before all who are potentially affected, even if some are "bothered." If during the US civil rights movement special buses had been designated as the only ones in which people could refuse to surrender their seats, little progress would have been made that way. (This is why many find disturbing the current practice by US authorities of cordoning off politically important meetings, and creating blocks away what are called "free speech zones.") All democracies, even workplace democracies, require public debate – sometimes even about bothersome issues.

I am not suggesting that dealing effectively with ethics requires a free-for-all. There is a difference between a debate and a riot. Indeed, leaders are in an ideal position to facilitate the former and help avoid the latter. Leadership has the power to foster (or undermine) the presence of appropriate infrastructures that make public discussion of ethics possible. These can take the form of regular or special meetings, email lists, newsletters, public squares, hallway conversations, public access media, the sidewalk in front of city hall, and so on. The idea is that their presence and purpose be known by everyone involved and that anyone can have access to them to express ethical concerns, debate issues or make a protest. It is the responsibility of leadership to assure that controversy is not a riot and to know when ethical discussions call for their guidance and when they do not. In the case above, I can only wish that the senior manager's boss had taken him aside and said, "Next time, don't interfere."

WHEN LEADERS UNDERSTEER THE SYSTEM: ENGAGING VALUES INFRASTRUCTURES

Just as human systems have technological infrastructures, both artifactual and human systems have what I call "values infrastructures." A values infrastructure is made up out of what is valuable to individuals and groups about themselves, the physical and social spaces within which they live and work, the various means that they employ to do what they do, and so on.[15] Among what people find valuable are things that can have a positive or negative impact on the wellbeing of themselves and others. That is, ethics is part of what people find valuable and is thus part of their values infrastructure.

Getting a sense of an individual's or group's values infrastructure can be easier than it might seem. I have found that if you ask people what their ethics or values are, they are often uncomfortable. But if you ask what is valuable to them about their job or the spaces in which they live and work or their associations with other people, an interesting and useful conversation often ensues. And if they can show you, or you can observe, examples of this in the course of their actual work practice or social interactions, the picture of the values infrastructure can become even more robust.

The importance of values infrastructures to work practice and leadership can be seen in the case of a project team I observed in a high-tech research and development laboratory. The team was developing a computer conferencing application that included, along with audio and video connections, the components of a "virtual office." The aim was to make it possible for each user to create a virtual office on his or her computer by setting up the virtual equivalent of pieces of typical office equipment, such as a whiteboard, a filing cabinet, a book case, and so on.

The team leader decided early on that the application should be as flexible as possible so each end-user could have a virtual office that fitted his or her individual needs and style. I spoke at length with him concerning this, and quickly learned that he was passionate about the application's flexibility. He gave maximization of flexibility as a reason for his design choices at all levels of the application – from the interface, to the architecture, and even to writing the software code. I asked him in various ways why flexibility was so important to him. He indicated repeatedly that he was committed to "empowering the user" and he ultimately described this in terms of workplace democracy. Flexibility, user empowerment and workplace democracy emerged as values that guided his work. And he and his team literally built these values into the technology.[16] I mean "literally" in the sense that one could not explain why the application had certain technical characteristics that it did without reference to those values.

The virtual office application was tested by installing it on the computers of a group of support staff in the lab. Although the group had been eager to be part of the test, once the application was installed, they made little use of it. In fact, they hardly configured their "virtual offices" at all. Whatever else this may have indicated, it meant that they took almost no advantage of the flexibility that the team leader had worked so hard and passionately to have his team create. At this stage, the application looked like a potential failure.

When I asked the support staff members about the test, they said that they felt "abandoned." From their perspective, the project team came in, installed the application and went away. They had wanted more guidance and help from them. In further discussions with members of this group, I learned that among the things that were valuable to them about their work were feeling included and supported.

This, I concluded, was a source of the problem. The virtual office application, as an artifactual system, had the values of the project team and its leader built into it. But the project team and the staff group, as human systems, had different values infrastructures. Flexibility for the user clashed with wanting to feel supported. Consequently, what was intended as democratic empowerment was taken as abandonment. The values at play were all at root ethical in character because they related to the wellbeing in the people involved. So, the problem encountered in testing the application was not technological as much as it was ethical. In untangling the problem it seemed essential to me to recognize that no amount of adjusting the artifactual system alone would address the whole of the situation. It was also important to deal with the clash of values infrastructures at the level of the human systems. In fact, this surfaced when the two groups later began to talk with one another. The staff came to understand that the developers had intended the flexibility to put more power in their hands (even though it ended up being technically more than they felt comfortable with). The value that the staff members placed on being supported in dealing with new workplace technologies, meanwhile, quickly came to the attention of the project team leader. It became clear that this was a case in which the leader needed to give more direction not less. He was then able to plan the next phase of the project to include more follow-through support for the staff while still incorporating some flexibility into the design of the application.

MISLABELING SYSTEMS: OR THE FALLACY OF COUNTERFEIT NATURALISM

Leadership as the stewardship of systems with a moral dimension applies not only to cases of single or local systems but also, importantly, to broader public contexts. Leaders have particular and important roles to play in how we all address ethical issues within the network of governmental, economic and social institutions that increasingly pervade and support our public lives.[17] These leadership roles, however, are often curtailed by the very way we talk about and understand the systems we depend upon. An important example of this is what I call the fallacy of "counterfeit naturalism."

It is a conceptual and practical mistake to treat an artifactual or human system as if it were a natural one. Nonetheless, this is often done. In a recent National Public Radio interview, for example, a noted economist said, "jobs, like water, naturally flow downhill to the cheapest provider." Technically speaking, however, there is nothing "natural" about this at all. Economies and job markets are not part of nature, they are systems created by people. The way jobs "flow" is a result of how we design the systems they are part of. Treating artifactual and human systems as natural ones amounts to "counterfeit naturalism." If "naturalism" can be defined as understanding something in natural terms (lightning, for example, as being caused by weather conditions rather than by Zeus), then "counterfeit naturalism" would mean understand as natural something that is not, particularly when this can be misleading. In this respect, counterfeit naturalism entails at least two major pitfalls bearing on leadership and ethics.

First, the more we engage in counterfeit naturalism, the more likely we are to diagnose problems and design solutions that may be appropriate to natural systems but not to artifactual or human ones. If leaders think of the flow of jobs to the cheapest provider as natural, it could make sense to promote governmental or corporate policies designed to avoid interference with this "natural" process. (Indeed, this can even include an implicit sense of "natural" standing in for "good.") On the other hand, if leaders think of this in terms of systems we have made, it could make more sense to consider policies that aim to redirect or curtail that flow.

The second issue derives from the fact that we generally do not see ethics as part of natural systems. We may hold ourselves responsible for how we treat nature, but we do not find ethics at work within nature itself. No one holds hurricanes morally responsible for the damage they cause. We do, however, hold people morally responsible for what they do with the aid of tools or teams. So counterfeit naturalism undermines leadership's ability to deal appropriately and effectively with the ethical aspects of human and artifactual systems because it treats them as systems, like hurricanes, with no obvious ethical dimension. If the flow of jobs is taken to be a natural occurrence, it could make no more sense for leaders to debate the ethics of it than to debate the ethics of the tides.

This is also seen when leaders justify their choices by making claims like "we are going with what works" or "my opponent's plan won't work." Comments such as these point to the instrumental aspects of human and artifactual systems, but suggest that, like natural systems, they are without an ethical dimension. By appealing only to the instrumental, they obscure the role that ethics plays in shaping both the choices leaders make and the consequences of those choices. Leadership choices are never solely about what will and will not work. They are also always about the aims one wants to further and what one considers appropriate ways of furthering them. Keeping the discussion at the level of what supposedly will and will not work misses – or dodges – the need to deal effectively with the ethics inherent in all leadership choices.

Leaders, as stewards of systems with an inescapable moral dimension, have the responsibility for enabling and encouraging the people they lead to engage moral issues in their own right. Counterfeit naturalism frustrates that responsibility by treating governmental, economic and social systems as if their moral dimension does not exist and by proposing diagnoses and solutions that may not be appropriate to non-natural systems. How our institutions function is an issue of crucial public importance, especially with respect to how they address issues of moral concern. Effective and responsible handling of such moral concerns calls for public discourse about them. Leaders in relevant areas such as government, industry, and community advocacy have a powerful role to play in enabling and directing the character of that discourse.

CONCLUSION: THE PRACTICALITY OF ETHICS

If, like Thoreau, I were to allow myself to make an idealistic proposal with the intent that it point to an utterly practical lesson, it would be that absolutely all considerations of "effective leadership" should be replaced with considerations of "ethical leadership." In the long run, the two ought to be the same. The reason for preferring one term over the other would be the immediacy with which it invites moral consideration. The impact systems have, for good or ill, on the wellbeing of those within and around them is amplified by the power and influence vested in the leaders of those systems. Consideration of the wellbeing of others is at the core of ethics. Undermining the wellbeing of the governed undermines systemic stability and sustenance, and thus undermines the ability to govern. In practical terms, that which governs best, governs ethically.

Leaders are in a unique position to signal that assessing the ethical aspects of such topics as those touched on above is desirable and practical. Leaders must be given and must assume the responsibility to make ethical assessments at the systemic level and not just at the level of "bad apples." Leaders have a primary responsibility to provide and maintain infrastructures that make public discussions of ethics possible, and to safeguard their appropriateness to the human systems in which they function. Perhaps more than anyone else, leaders can help assure that ethical discussions are open to all who are affected by the issues they concern. And they can help others recognize that those issues are sometimes "controversial" and that they are never about whether or not an artifactual or human system "works" but about *how* we want it to work and what ends we want it to serve. We need to be able to rely on our leaders to exercise a keen sense of when the ethical workings of a system call for their intervention and when it is best that they "don't interfere." Leaders have the power to help assure that public moral discourse is not foreclosed through the fallacious characterization of social, political and economic systems as natural. Finally, effective leadership ought to reflect the fact that the systems leaders are in charge of are ones of our own making that have a deep and abiding ethical dimension deserving of their stewardship.

NOTES

1. Portions of the research that contributed to the writing of this chapter were supported, in part, by a grant from the National Science Foundation (#9320927).
2. Thoreau, Henry David, "Civil Disobedience" in *Civil Disobedience, Solitude and Life Without Principle*, Amherst, NY: Prometheus Books, 1998 [orig. 1848].
3. Previn, André, *No Minor Chords: My Days in Hollywood*, New York: Doubleday, 1991, p. 50.
4. Wiener, Norbert, *Cybernetics: or Control and Communication in the Animal and the Machine*, Cambridge, MA: MIT Press, 1962 [orig. 1948].
5. Bertalanffy, Ludwig von, *General System Theory: Foundations, Development and Applications*, New York: George Braziller, 1968.
6. See, for example, Emery, F. and Trist, E., "Socio-Technical Systems," in *Management Sciences, Models, and Techniques*, volume 2, Churchman, C.W. and Verhulst, M. (eds), Oxford: Pergamon, 1960; Beer, Stafford, *Brain of the Firm*, Hoboken, NJ: John Wiley & Sons; 2nd edition, 1994 [orig. 1972]; Simon, Herbert A., *The Sciences of the Artificial*, Cambridge, MA: MIT Press; 3rd edition, 1996; and March, James G. and Simon, Herbert A., *Organizations*, Cambridge, MA: Basil Blackwell, 1993.

7. See especially, Bateson, Gregory, *Steps to an Ecology of Mind*, New York: Ballantine Books; Reissue edition, 1990 [orig. 1972]; and Bateson, Gregory, *Mind and Nature: A Necessary Unity (Advances in Systems Theory, Complexity, and the Human Sciences)*, Cresskill, NJ: Hampton Press, Incorporated, 2002 [orig. 1979].
8. Vickers, Sir Geoffrey, *Human Systems Are Different*, London: Harper & Row, Publishers, 1983; and Vickers, Sir Geoffrey, *The Art of Judgment: A Study of Policy Making*, Thousand Oaks: Sage Publications, 1996 [orig. 1965].
9. Arendt, Hannah, *The Human Condition*, Chicago: University of Chicago Press, 1998 [orig. 1958], page 7.
10. Huxley, Thomas H., "Evolution and Ethics [1893]," in *Evolution and Ethics and other Essays*, Honolulu: University Press of the Pacific, 2002 [orig. 1896].
11. Dewey, John, *Logic: The Theory of Inquiry*, New York: Henry Holt and Company, 1938; and Burke, Tom, *Dewey's New Logic: A Reply to Russell*, Chicago: University of Chicago Press, 1994.
12. Cook, S.D. Noam and Brown, John Seely, "Bridging Epistemologies: The Generative Dance Between Organizational Knowledge and Organizational Knowing," *Organizational Science*, Volume 10, Number 4, July–August, 1999.
13. Cook, S.D. Noam. "Autonomy, Interdependence, and Moral Governance: Pluralism in a Rocking Boat," in *Rethinking Public Policy-Making: Questioning Assumptions, Challenging Beliefs*, Blunden, Margaret and Dando, Malcolm (eds), London: Sage Publications, 1995.
14. Cook, S.D. Noam and Yanow, D.J., "Culture and Organizational Learning," *Journal of Management Inquiry*, Volume 2, Issue 4, December 1993.
15. Schein, Edgar H., *Organizational Culture and Leadership* (third edition), San Francisco, CA: Jossey-Bass, 2004 [orig. 1985].
16. Winner, Langdon, "Do Artifacts Have Politics?" in *The Whale and the Reactor: A Search for Limits in an Age of High Technology*, Chicago: University of Chicago Press, 1986.
17. Cook, S.D. Noam and Wagenaar, Hendrik, "Understanding Policy Practices: Action, Dialectic and Deliberation in Policy Analysis," in *Deliberative Policy Analysis: Understanding Governance in the Network Society*, Maarten Hajer and Hendrik Wagenaar (eds), New York: Cambridge University Press, 2003.

9. Expanding the horizons of leadership

Norman E. Bowie

What makes a great leader in business? Most of the answers to this question focus on the financial results obtained. This is the criterion that is used in Jim Collins's *Good to Great*, a book that is much quoted in leadership circles.[1] I maintain that superior financial results are not enough. First, borrowing an idea that is well established in the European Union, the successful business leader should lead a successful, sustainable corporation. Specifically, the successful business leader must achieve superior financial results, superior results in protecting the environment, and superior results in providing for corporate social responsibility. Second, if the conclusion supported by the anecdotal information I provide can be established through rigorous social science methods, the successful business leader should have integrity in both his business life and his personal life. When these additional criteria are used to define successful business leadership, we find that the number of great business leaders is actually quite small.

GREAT BUSINESS LEADERS MUST BUILD SUCCESSFUL SUSTAINABLE CORPORATIONS

I do not think being the CEO of a "great" company in Collins's sense is sufficient for genuine leadership or leadership in the best sense. The European Union does not view the function of the corporation as maximizing shareholder value. Rather, it argues that the corporation should be managed in a way that makes it sustainable as determined by financial success, environmental friendliness, and social responsibility – the three pillars of sustainability. According to a 1987 report by the World Commission on Environment and Development, "Sustainable development is development that meets the needs of the present without compromising the ability of future generations to meet their own needs."[2] The three pillars of sustainability are measured by triple bottom-line accounting. The goal of the European Union is "to become the most competitive and dynamic knowledge-based economy in the world, capable of sustainable economic growth with more and better jobs and greater social cohesion."[3] The European Union spelled out a strategy for corporate social responsibility (dubbed CSR Europe) in one of its so-called Green Paper publications:

> Corporate social responsibility is essentially a concept whereby companies decide voluntarily to contribute to a better society and a cleaner environment. At a time when the European Union endeavours to identify its common values by adopting a Charter of Fundamental Rights, an increasing number of European companies recognise their social responsibility more and more clearly and consider it as part of their identity. This responsibility is expressed towards employees and more generally towards all the stakeholders affected by business and which in turn can influence its success.[4]

As stipulated in the Green Paper, corporate social responsibility extends beyond mere compliance with legal expectations to emphasize investing in human capital, the environment, and relations with stakeholders. The internal dimension of corporate social responsibility includes enlightened human resources management, such as a concern with lifelong learning; health and safety at work; helping workers adapt to change; and more friendly management of environmental outcomes and natural resources. The external dimension includes promotion of CSR throughout the supply chain, a commitment to human rights, and a commitment to sustainable global development.

Despite the generalities of CSR language, it is nevertheless not language that is common in American business circles. I have never read an article on leadership by an American author that argues that a genuine business leader must be committed to and achieve corporate sustainability. If these responsibilities were recognized as legitimate responsibilities of business, the demands for successful business leadership would be much greater.

When I attended an international business ethics seminar in Europe recently, I noticed that the term *corporate responsibility* is replacing the term *corporate social responsibility* and that *corporate responsibility* is being equated with *sustainability* in the United Kingdom. UK firms committed to sustainability include British American Tobacco, GlaxoSmithKline, Rio Tinto, BP (formerly known as British Petroleum), and Shell (a UK–Dutch company). Each year, the Association of Chartered Certified Accountants in the United Kingdom gives awards for sustainability reporting. In 2003, there were 22 short-listed reports and 12 awards. The European Union continues to do research and publish reports on corporate social responsibility, but the language of sustainability is widely used on the Continent as well. I have chosen to state my basic thesis of this section in the language of sustainability.

Given that the European Union seems to accept and expect corporate social responsibility and sustainability to be the modus operandi, its business leaders will be held to a higher standard than leaders in the United States both in practice and in publications such as *Good to Great* that critique good leadership.

But why should the United States adopt this foreign definition of business strategy and thus of business leadership? If the European Union strategy proved economically superior to the American strategy, there would be a pragmatic reason to adopt the European Union strategy. The European Union clearly believes in the long-term superiority of the philosophy of corporate social responsibility, making the case for it in the Green Paper thus: "A number of companies with good social and environmental records indicate that these activities can result in better performance and can generate more profits and growth."[5] Whether the European Union can outperform the United States in the long run, however, is uncertain. Most American commentators believe not. Indeed, many believe that a commitment to corporate social responsibility weakens economic growth rather than enabling it. Time will tell.

The other argument for adopting this "foreign" concept of responsible business leadership is normative or moral. A notion of leadership that measures legitimacy on achieving sustainability, rather than simply financial success, is morally superior.

A brief review of theories of the purpose of the firm may be in order here. The classical view most clearly articulated by Nobel Prize-winning economist Milton Friedman argues that the purpose of the firm is to maximize profit for stockholders. In this view, managers and boards of public corporations are merely agents of the stockholders. Thus, for Friedman, the sole social responsibility of business is to be as profitable as possible within the confines of law and ordinary morality. The best-known opposing view is the stakeholder theory, championed in academic business ethics by R. Edward Freeman. In stakeholder theory, the purpose of the firm is to balance the needs and interests of the legitimate stakeholders. In the narrow sense, stakeholder groups are defined as those groups whose support is necessary if the firm is to survive. Firms committed to sustainability engage in dialogue with stakeholders as a means of determining policy. Thus, such firms are committed to stakeholder theory rather than stockholder theory.

Several books on the topic of business ethics make the case for the superiority of stakeholder theory over stockholder theory. Business ethics critics have raised objections to Friedman's view that emphasizes shareholder wealth above all else. Friedman's view may still dominate the business school curriculum, but other models are rapidly surpassing it in the real world of business – at least in public relations statements.

Interestingly, Freeman and his colleagues and students, while upholding the moral superiority of stakeholder theory over stockholder theory, nevertheless note that one of the main challenges to stakeholder theory is its impracticality. They believe it is impossible to take into account and balance the diverse needs of the various corporate stakeholders. They view the suggestion that a corporation should actually engage its stakeholders in dialogue with intense skepticism, arguing that nothing would ever get accomplished and business would bog down in endless hours of debate without any consensus ever being reached. Despite the theoretical appeal of Freeman's argument, business practice has shown it to be spurious. In point of fact, stakeholder dialogue is the preferred means for managing sustainability. For example, BP and Shell have engaged in extensive stakeholder dialogues as they seek agreement on pipeline construction in underdeveloped countries and on the lands of indigenous people. And British American Tobacco has similarly engaged in extensive stakeholder dialogues as it wrestles with the health issues surrounding smoking.

Discussions of sustainability are beginning to appear in the business ethics literature, especially by scholars who belong to the European Business Ethics Network. As yet, however, there has been little crossover from the business ethics literature into the leadership literature. A commitment to stakeholder management is not a requirement for being on the list of great business leaders. Philip Morris, for example, made the list of best companies in Collins's book *Good to Great*. But is the CEO of Philip Morris a great leader? Many answer in the negative simply because Philip Morris sells tobacco. Most social responsibility investment screens eliminate tobacco companies. After visiting British American Tobacco, which is trying to be a sustainable corporation, I am no longer certain of the fairness of this type of screening policy. However, I do not detect a commitment to sustainability from Philip Morris, which is still stuck in a philanthropic model of social responsibility to be discussed below.

Jim Collins prepared a special article for the July 21, 2003, issue of *Fortune* titled "The 10 Greatest CEOs of All Time." It was a fascinating list. Several of the top ten were what I call stakeholder or sustainability CEOs. I count Hewlett-Packard co-founder David Packard, former Johnson & Johnson CEO James Burke, and George Merck of Merck & Company (who specifically put profit second) as stakeholder managers. None of those listed had ever been the CEO of an American automobile company. Henry Ford was not on the list. Nor was Jack Welch, former CEO of General Electric. But the first president of General Electric, Charles Coffin, was. Indeed, Collins gave him the highest ranking. Collins, however, did not base his rankings on a commitment to stakeholder management. Instead, Collins ranked Charles Coffin number one because he "built the stage on which they all played"; Bill Allen of Boeing number two because he "thought bigger"; Wal-Mart founder Sam Walton number three because he "overcame his charisma"; and Kimberly-Clark chief Darwin Smith number five because he "asked questions and moved rocks."[6]

Using this discussion as a teaser, make up your own list of the ten greatest American CEOs. What criteria would you use? If you use "successfully promoting the interests of all the stakeholders" or the European phrase "successfully achieved sustainability," who would be on your list? What I have been arguing for is the moral superiority of a list that uses such criteria. I also believe, as do many CEOs, that there is a plausible business case to be made for sustainability.

Before leaving this topic, some reference should be made to corporate and individual charity. Many American business leaders think of social responsibility in terms of charity – of giving money away either directly or through a corporate foundation. Target, for example, gives 5 percent of its pretax income to charity. Charitable giving has been a hallmark of the business community in Minneapolis-St Paul where Target has its headquarters. Advocates of Milton Friedman's position abhor such charitable giving. They consider it tantamount to theft or, perhaps more kindly put, as taxation without representation. That charge seems overblown. If persons who buy Target stock are not well aware of Target's policy of giving back to the community, they should be. People who own Target stock either endorse Target's program of corporate giving or they believe that it has either a neutral or positive effect with respect to Target's profits. Alternatively, some CEOs give away their own money rather than that of the corporation. Bill Gates (operating through the Bill and Melinda Gates Foundation) and Ted Turner come to mind. Must a business leader be a leader in giving to charity? If the answer to that question is yes, does it matter if it is individual charity or corporate charity?

Since I endorse stakeholder management or sustainability, I think the leaders of corporations have a responsibility to be leaders in the community as well. In other words, a great business leader should have a sense of social responsibility. However, a business leader might choose to exercise his or her social responsibility in a number of ways. He can give personally, or he can give through his corporate foundation. He can also encourage the company to give to charity either directly or through a corporate foundation.

I am not particularly concerned with the method of giving. I wish to defend a more radical thesis. Individual or corporate charity as it has been practiced in the United States is no longer enough. I maintain that there is more to corporate social responsibility than charity. First, business must address the problems it helps create. A firearms manufacturer, for example, has an obligation to fund education on the safe handling of firearms. Second, companies should concentrate on social problems where their resources or technical expertise can have the greatest impact. A pharmaceutical company that gives money to a symphony but ignores the question of whether it should reduce the price of its AIDS medication for patients in Africa is not being sufficiently socially responsible. I am not in any way saying that the pharmaceutical company is to blame for the problem. Rather, I am making a point about efficiency. Companies should spend their scarce resources where they can do the most good. Thus, I am saying that the object of charity matters. If a company is even in part the cause of the problem, regardless of whether it is to blame or not, its first obligation is to help clean up that problem. Secondly, a company should get the biggest bang for its buck by contributing to solving social problems where it has either special resources or special expertise.

But that is not all. As previously discussed, the European definition of corporate leadership requires taking a stand on certain social issues. The issues need not involve charity at all. For example, nearly all European companies that commit to sustainability also commit to supporting the UN Declaration of Human Rights, both in their own business and in the business activities of their supply chains. Seldom if ever does an American company make such a commitment to the UN Declaration as part of its statement of business purpose. Let me make the point in another way: corporate social responsibility requires that the business leader make sure that his business activities do not violate human rights. He also has some responsibility to see that his stakeholders, particularly suppliers, do not violate human rights. For example, Nike and Adidas have accepted this responsibility with respect to their suppliers. Finally, and perhaps most controversial of all, corporations need to resist clear violations of human rights by the governments of the countries where they do business. If they do not wish to accept this obligation, then they should not be doing business in countries with an extensive record of human rights abuses. The Sullivan Principles, which established a code of conduct for human rights and equal opportunity for companies operating in South Africa during apartheid, were based on this moral obligation. Also, Royal Dutch Shell changed its policy with respect to intervention in political affairs when it was roundly criticized internationally for not intervening to save the life of writer and activist Ken Saro-Wiwa. Saro-Wiwa was executed in 1995 by the Nigerian government for his part in organizing the Orgoni people to protest against the pollution and unfair labor practices resulting from Shell's oil drilling in the Niger Delta. The issues discussed in this section illustrate why successful corporate leadership requires corporate social responsibility, not simply individual corporate charity.

One final point about the leader of a sustainable corporation needs to be made. Insistence that ethical leadership requires a commitment to sustainability has considerable impact on our expectations of a genuine leader, since ethical leadership is a necessary condition for genuine leadership.

What would we expect the personality or character of the leader of a sustainable corporation to be? It seems to me that the leader of a sustainable corporation is not likely to be a highly charismatic person or to be a media star along the lines of Jack Welch. First of all, sustainability cannot be achieved by dramatic actions such as the massive downsizing Welch implemented at General Electric, earning him the nickname Neutron Jack. Second, commitment to the environment and to social responsibility requires a kind of empathy and social concern that is not often seen in leaders known for highly publicized financial turn-arounds. The leaders of the sustainable corporation are not likely to be captains of industry in the traditional sense. But don't we need ruthless leaders for financial success? With one notable exception, I think the empirical evidence from organizational behavior is to answer the question in the negative. Only if a company is in trouble because it is bloated and has lost its way with respect to mission and values might a ruthless CEO help. Normally the ruthless leader destroys employee morale and, thus, productivity and customer relations.

If the ruthless leader is not the answer, what is? I think the successful leader of a sustainable corporation will fit the model of the successful leader in *Good to Great*. I am critical of that book, not because I disagree with Collins's list of characteristics of the leader who takes a firm from good to great, but because I think Collins's conception of success is too narrow. The leader of the good-to-great corporation has two important characteristics – personal humility and tremendous resolve.[7] It is the characteristic of humility that I find especially fascinating for this study. Collins documents the humility of the good-to-great leader in a number of ways. First, Collins names these leaders and then points out that it is unlikely that we have ever heard of any of them. Second, Collins points out that these leaders have adopted the principle of the window and the mirror. According to that principle, when things go right, the leader looks out the window to see who made it happen. On the other hand, when things go wrong, the leader looks in the mirror to see what mistakes he or she made.[8] It is this type of person, rather than the Jack Welch type, who is most likely to be a successful leader of a sustainable corporation. At least that is what I would hypothesize. It would be interesting to have an empirical study looking at the leaders of European corporations who are practicing sustainability to see if my hypothesis can be borne out. In proposing this hypothesis, I recognize that most people do not act by the principle of the window and the mirror. In fact, they usually behave in the exact opposite way. But if Collins is right, that is why they are not leaders. Successful leaders need to adopt ways of behaving that are different from the crowd. That is what makes them leaders.

These remarks on personality or character provide a segue to the next section. I have come to the conclusion that the personality or overall character of a leader is important in determining whether or not he should be described as an ethical leader. As I argue in the next section, I think the great ethical leader should be ethical in all parts of his life. Of course, personal ethics requires that. But I am arguing for a positive correlation between the quality of a person's ethics in his or her personal life and the quality of his or her business ethics. If I am right here, then a high level of personal ethics becomes a requirement of business ethics.

GREAT LEADERS MUST HAVE PERSONAL INTEGRITY

Philosopher Joanne Ciulla has indicated that the question of leadership is the question of whether an immoral person like Hitler can be described as a leader.[9] This question can itself be subdivided into two questions. Can a person who is immoral in the area where he or she is a leader be a genuine leader? Can a person who is immoral in areas where he or she is not a leader be a genuine leader? Hitler illustrates the former category, and perhaps Bill Clinton represents the latter category. I am not comparing Clinton to Hitler. Indeed, as a liberal Democrat, I took the view that the fact that Clinton was unfaithful to his wife on multiple occasions and lied about it did not diminish his leadership as president. For example, it did not affect his leadership in trying to settle the conflict between the Israelis and the Palestinians. However, as I learn more and more about those involved in corporate scandals, I am discovering that people who were unethical in business were also unethical in other aspects of their lives. In others words, when we know that a person is a liar and cheat in his or her personal life, we might predict that he or she will be unethical as a business leader. My evidence at this point is anecdotal, but I think it is strong enough to argue for some sophisticated empirical research on the topic. And if the social science research supports the anecdotal evidence, then I would argue that a genuine leader ought to have high personal integrity in all aspects of his or her life.

Before making my case, a few caveats are in order. I agree with Joanne Ciulla that a great leader must be effective as well as ethical.[10] Thus, in business an ethical leader who leads his or her company into bankruptcy cannot qualify as a great leader. William Norris, founder of computer company Control Data in Minneapolis, was widely recognized as a highly moral CEO but also one who could not manage the company in a way to keep it on a sound financial basis. Personal integrity is a necessary condition for a great business leader; it is not a sufficient one.

Second, I admit that many will support an unethical leader and follow him or her if it is in their interest. Ciulla reports that after Trent Lott made insensitive racial comments, many of his African-American constituents indicated that they would still support him. Lott had used his seniority and influence in Congress to bring money and jobs to his state. As Ciulla said, "In politics, the old saying 'He may be a son of a bitch, but he's *our* son of a bitch,' captures the trade-off between ethics and effectiveness. In other words, as long as Lott gets the job done, we do not care about his ethics."[11]

Third, I think most people weigh the risk versus the potential gain more than they are willing to admit when deciding whether to do something immoral. For example, most people would not steal a few dollars even if they were very unlikely to get caught; however, many more would steal a million dollars if the risk factors remained the same. Be that as it may, character still matters. A person who has honesty as an integral part of his or her character is far less likely to steal a million dollars than someone who doesn't.

I also agree with Ciulla that leaders may be subject to greater temptations than many of us. After all, they have a great amount of power and are used to getting their way. They are tempted to think they are above the law and above the ethical standards that govern mere mortals.[12]

Dean Ludwig and Clinton Longenecker have referred to this kind of behavior as the Bathsheba Syndrome. The name is taken from the Old Testament story where King David engages in an adulterous relationship with Bathsheba, gets her pregnant, and eventually orders her husband, Uriah, to the front lines of battle where he is killed. I assume Ludwig and Longenecker use this story to show that as power and success increase, so too does the probability that a person's character will suffer.[13] I have observed this phenomenon firsthand.

Although the temptations are real, should the behavior be excused? In an important paper that elaborates and modifies the Ludwig and Longenecker research, Terry Price argues that leaders sometimes behave unethically because they think they are special and justified in their deviations.[14] But I wonder whether they should be excused based on this belief. Leaders do think they are special. If they are correct in this belief, they need to be special in avoiding temptations that the rest of us do not face.[15] Let us consider some actual examples.

THE NEGATIVE CASE

Consider the people who have been at the center of various scandals in business who have had morally problematic personal lives as well. As this article goes to press, I just saw an announcement for a new book by Christopher Byron, *Testosterone Inc.* Apparently this book looks into the lives of CEOs Jack Welch of General Electric, Ronald Perelman of Revlon, Al Dunlap of Sunbeam, and Dennis Kozlowski of Tyco and finds that these men were obsessed with sex and "drunk on power and addicted to fame."[16] In other words, they possessed vices that were marks of their character. Your character does not change as you move from one area of your life to another. The cases I enumerate below illustrate that it is difficult to have a schizophrenic character – ethical in one part of your life and unethical in another. I am not claiming that unethical conduct in one area causes unethical conduct in another; and I certainly would not know whether it is lack of ethics in business that causes lack of ethics in one's personal life or the other way around. I am hypothesizing that there is a positive correlation between ethical or unethical behavior in business and ethical or unethical behavior in one's personal life. Let us examine the lives of a few of those behind corporate scandals in more detail.

1. The Haft Family and Dart Drug Stores

The Haft family, who operated under the retail holding company Dart Group Corporation, targeted the Dayton Hudson Company (the name of the parent company for the Target retail chain at the time) for takeover in 1987. The Hafts had attempted a number of takeovers of Dayton Hudson before and had been paid greenmail to go away. The Dayton Hudson Company was considered a pillar of the community in Minnesota, giving 5 percent of its pretax profits to charity, for example. The Hafts' drugstore chain, Dart Drug, on the other hand, was not known for its enlightened management or its charitable contributions. At the end of a Harvard Business School video case on Dayton Hudson, the Dayton Hudson public relations spokesman summarized how he and the company were able to get the Minnesota legislature to go into special session and pass an anti-takeover bill that saved Dayton Hudson. He said, "Have the most revered corporate citizen as your client, the most hated manager as your opponent, and get the hell out of the way." In October of 1987, the Dart Company was found to be in violation of the security laws.

As with so many cases of fallen executives, the Hafts had a reputation for lavish lifestyles, both individually and collectively. Some critics considered Ronald Haft, youngest son of business tycoon Herbert Haft, a playboy who spent much of his time enjoying himself in his two luxurious homes in California. When a major rift developed between Herbert Haft and his wife, Gloria, eldest son, Robert, and daughter, Linda, Ronald began spending much more time in his Washington, DC, home in order to manage the family real estate holdings in metro Washington. Later the Haft family became totally dysfunctional, and Herbert Haft divorced Gloria. In a vicious battle over the empire, Robert and Linda allied themselves with their mother, while Ronald supported his father. For example, Ronald defended his father when his mother accused Herbert of physical and mental abuse. For their part, Gloria, Robert, and Linda accused Ronald of drilling open a family safe-deposit box without their knowledge and taking documents belonging to them. They also accused him of using the power of attorney of his mother to "launder" money. Gloria and Ronald eventually stopped speaking to each other.[17] In 1994 a court ordered Herbert Haft to pay his son Robert more than $34 million in a wrongful termination suit.[18] Around the same time, Herbert Haft's relationship with son Ronald soured, and father and youngest son headed for the courtrooms. At this point, the Haft patriarch was only communicating with family members through lawyers.[19] Family relations were still frosty in 1999 when Herbert Haft and Robert Haft launched competing Internet vitamin sales operations in the

Washington, DC area.[20] Although family members claimed to be making some attempt at reconciliation at the time of Herbert Haft's death on September 1, 2004, they were still embroiled in familial legal disputes in the courts.[21]

2. "Chainsaw" Al Dunlap, former CEO of Scott Paper and Sunbeam

The title of Al Dunlap's book, *Mean Business*, sums up his business approach. A couple of quotations from the book give you the flavor of his personal philosophy: "If you want a friend, get a dog."[22] "You cannot overpay a good CEO. . . . Even though I walked away from Scott more than $100 million richer then when I arrived, I was still the biggest bargain in Corporate America."[23] I recall one business trade publication commenting on the fact that Dunlap had a dysfunctional family life. Basically, his family disliked him as much as many in the business community disliked him.

3. Martha Stewart and ImClone Insider Trading

Martha Stewart has not been implicated or even rumored to be involved in a sex scandal. Moreover, although she is certainly acquisitive and materialistic, she may not have crossed the line into greed. However, Stewart has a long and extensive reputation as being unpleasant. The word that best describes Stewart, according to one source, rhymes with *witch*. Stewart also has a bad habit of being extremely arrogant and of playing fast and loose with the truth. It is widely believed that her reputation may have influenced the jury in her obstruction-of-justice trial. It is also well known that she could have avoided trial and a prison term altogether if she had simply told the truth initially to government prosecutors. As a result of her trial and subsequent conviction, the financial future of her company was in doubt. Character and reputation in one's personal life do have an impact on a business. The odd twist to her story is that her company's stock went up when she was released from jail. The public seems more sympathetic to a chastened Stewart.

4. Dennis Kozlowski and Tyco

Dennis Kozlowski, former CEO of Tyco, has come to symbolize the life of excess. It is common knowledge that he has been indicted for tax evasion. What is interesting about Kozlowski is the clear connection between personal excess and misconduct in business. During his trial, the jury viewed a video-tape of the birthday party Kozlowski threw for his wife. Tyco allegedly paid half the $2 million bill for the weeklong birthday bash in Sardinia. During the extravaganza, vodka flowed freely from the penis of an ice sculpture of Michelangelo's David and sparklers erupted from the breasts of the birthday cake shaped as a naked woman.[24] Surely spending Tyco's money on such a party is a violation of shareholder rights. Kozlowski's current legal difficulties indicate he is paying a price for his unethical and illegal actions. Pity the man. He had to abort at least one of his projects – the building of a yacht by Derecktor Shipyards. Kozlowski had already spent $7.3 million on the sailboat's construction, less than half of the total sticker price of $17.8 million.[25]

5. Philip Condit and Boeing

A December 2003 article in *BusinessWeek* reported some of the recent scandals involving the Boeing Corporation. I will refer only to the ethical issues, not the management mistakes, mentioned in the article: Boeing paid $92.5 million to shareholders who accused the company of accounting irregularities. A class-action sex-discrimination suit was filed against Boeing. The Pentagon disciplined Boeing in July 2003 for possessing documents from rival Lockheed Martin. Boeing dismissed chief financial officer Michael Sears and manager Darleen Druyun in December 2003 for ethical misconduct in a scandal involving at least two multibillion-dollar aerospace defense contracts. The *BusinessWeek* article went on to describe CEO Philip Condit as having a reputation as a womanizer and an appetite for the high life. Married four times, he had Boeing's suite at the Four Seasons Olympic Hotel remodeled at company expense to serve as his private living quarters between two of his marriages. Under Condit's predecessor, Boeing had three small corporate jets. Under Condit, Boeing acquired a fleet of corporate jets, including one 737 decked out in English library style specifically for him. After his second marriage failed, he became romantically involved with a Boeing receptionist, Laverne Hawthorne. Several Boeing executives claim that Hawthorne filed a wrongful-termination suit and received a settlement when she was laid off shortly after breaking up with Condit.[26]

6. High Officials at Enron

Volumes have been written on Enron, but relatively little has been written on the personal ethics of some of the star players. A *Newsweek* article of March 11, 2002, provides an exception. As was the case with so many scandal-ridden companies, Enron executives were prone to excessive lifestyles, according to the *Newsweek* article. Formal Enron parties included Tiffany glassware as door prizes and waiters always at the ready with champagne. Former Enron CEO Jeffrey Skilling would reward his favorite employees with exotic trips. On one such trip to the Australian Outback, Enron people destroyed several rented SUVs. Informal Enron parties were even more excessive and included "luge shots" – cocktails poured over a block of ice straight into the mouth.

Enron executives were regulars at Treasures, a Houston strip club. On their lunch break, it was not unusual for Enron traders to buy a bottle of Cristal champagne costing as much as $575 and then retire to the VIP room at Treasures with some of the strippers.[27] The best-known frequenter of the strip clubs was Enron executive Lou Pai. Pai's expenses were so extravagant that they reached the attention of Enron founder Kenneth Lay, who sent out a memo indicating that Enron would no longer reimburse expenses at strip clubs. It is alleged that Pai had at least one tryst with two prostitutes at the Enron headquarters itself.[28]

As you would expect, extramarital sex was part of the mixture. Employees dubbed female coworkers whom they suspected were having affairs with their bosses "the French Lieutenants' Women." Pai married a former stripper after divorcing his wife.[29] Skilling himself divorced his wife and married an Enron accountant, Rebecca Carter. Skilling quickly promoted her to senior vice president and eventually to the company's 31-member Management Committee, where she was one of only five women. Shortly thereafter, Carter became Enron's corporate secretary.[30] Perhaps the most infamous affair was between top Enron executives Ken Rice and Amanda Martin. They made no attempt to keep their affair a secret. Public displays of affection were routine and often lewd. The glass walls of Martin's office provided optimal viewing for passers by to see the couple fondling each other.[31]

Interestingly, before coming to Enron, Lay had an extramarital affair with his secretary, whom he later married after divorcing his wife.[32] Once he came to Enron, however, Lay apparently did not engage in sexual misconduct. But he did permit and condone it – even when informed of specific instances and when threatened with legal action.[33] He certainly enjoyed a lavish lifestyle, including three homes in Aspen alone.[34] Robert Bryce put it this way:

> Although Ken Lay paid lip service to ethics and integrity, he had been compromised by his own past. As one former top-level Enron executive said, "Leaders cast shadows." And the shadow that Lay cast at Enron was that of a man who couldn't, or wouldn't, do anything to put a stop to the sexual misconduct.[35]

In addition to all this, Enron had a highly competitive individualistic culture with almost no formal controls. One can point out that this culture characterizes many firms and really should not count as unethical. True enough, but Enron really did carry this to an extreme. A *Wall Street Journal* report references a Lucite cube on chief financial officer Andrew Fastow's desk laying out Enron's values, including the company's view on communication: "When Enron says it's going to 'rip your face off,' . . . it will 'rip your face off.'"[36]

What is important for the thesis of this chapter is a perceived correlation between the sexual misconduct and the financial misconduct of Enron executives. Robert Bryce reports the following:

A Wall Street analyst who covered Enron for years said the sexual shenanigans at Enron became an important part of his take on the company and its financial statements. The analyst said when someone like Skilling, who has a wife and three kids and is heading a major company, starts sleeping around, "it addresses the character of the man. This is a guy who felt he could get away with anything. You saw it in his personal life and his business life."[37]

One member of Enron's executive committee put it this way:

The marital misconduct created an atmosphere where things had to be covered up. Having secrets, having things not be public, having things be suspected and not known, was a part of the deal. Everything at Enron was on a gradation scale. Are you cheating on your wife? Are you cheating in business? Where do you draw the line?[38]

Our anecdotal survey could go on and on. Yet another example is Bernie Ebbers, the former head of WorldCom. Ebbers enjoyed an extravagant lifestyle – one that apparently required substantial loans from WorldCom. Again, personal greed and business greed seemed to coexist in the same body. When things got tough, the decision to commit accounting fraud apparently came easily.

I admit that I have not done a good scientific study. That was not my intention. My intention was to provide sufficient evidence from popular press reports to focus attention on the extent to which misconduct in one's personal life is likely to be correlated with misconduct in one's business life. I think it would be interesting to do biographical studies of those at the center of corporate scandals to see to what extent lying and cheating are endemic in their personal lives as opposed to being limited to their business dealings. If serious biographical studies do suggest a positive correlation, then I think a serious social science study of the question would be warranted.

THE POSITIVE CASE

To make the positive case, we return once again to *Good to Great*. As you recall, humility was one of the main characteristics of the CEOs of all the great companies discussed in the book. Collins writes that humility + will = Level 5, with Level 5 referring to the highest possible level of executive capabilities.[39] Humility and excess do not often go together. The names of the CEOs of the great companies that appear on Collins's list are not likely to be familiar household names, the only possible exception being Cork Walgreen, since his surname is the same as the company name. Recall Collins's list of companies that transformed from good to great by following a certain pattern:

"fifteen-year cumulative stock returns at or below the general stock market, punctuated by a transition point, then cumulative returns at least three times the market over the next fifteen years."[40] Engineering that kind of turnaround requires a real leader. Although I have not read biographies of any of these people, I have certainly not seen their names on the gossip pages. The names of those remarkable leaders are George Cain of Abbott Laboratories, Alan Wurtzel of Circuit City, David Maxwell of Fannie Mae, Colman Mockler of Gillette, Darwin Smith of Kimberly-Clark, Jim Herring of Kroger, Lyle Everingham also of Kroger, Joe Cullman of Philip Morris, Fred Allen of Pitney Bowes, Cork Walgreen of Walgreens, and Carl Reichardt of Wells Fargo.[41]

As I pointed out earlier, one of the characteristics of the humble leader is that he or she looks out the window when things go right and looks in the mirror when things go wrong.[42] How many from our rogues gallery have taken that approach? I also am willing to propose the hypothesis that there is a low correlation between humility and lying and cheating. However I would like to see some hard data on this.

If the empirical evidence should bear me out, we need to expand our horizons on leadership. I think we must answer Ciulla's question in the affirmative: ethics is relevant in determining whether a so-called leader is a good leader. Hitler, for example, was not a good leader. But if the empirical data supports my hypothesis, we can go further: a person who is unethical in his or her personal life is likely to be unethical in business as well, and thus will not make a good business leader.

What conclusions can we draw from this analysis? At a time when leadership in corporate life seems to be at a low point, more and more is being demanded of business leaders if they are to be considered genuine leaders. In order to be financially successful and moral in managing the firm, a business leader must have high personal ethics and consider how he or she and the company can make a contribution to the greater good, thereby achieving sustainability.

Thus I have argued that the horizons of leadership must be expanded in two ways. First, genuine business leaders must be ethical in all aspects of their lives, including their personal lives. A major part of my argument for this contention is my hypothesis that there is a correlation between ethical behavior in business and ethical behavior in other aspects of one's life. Second, I have argued that one needs to adopt a philosophy of social responsibility if one is to be a genuine leader in business. If these arguments are accepted, then good leadership entails much more than has been traditionally recognized.

NOTES

1. Jim Collins, *Good to Great: Why Some Companies Make the Leap – and Others Don't* (New York: HarperBusiness, 2001).
2. World Commission on Environment and Development, *Our Common Future* (Oxford: Oxford University Press, 1987), 43.
3. Lisbon European Council, 23 and 24 March 2000, art. 5, sec. I, http://ue.eu.int/ueDocs/cms_Data/docs/pressData/en/ec/00100-r1.en0.htm.
4. European Commission, Directorate-General for Employment, "Green Paper: Promoting a European Framework for Corporate Social Responsibility," 5, http://europa.eu.int/comm/employment_social/soc-dial/csr/greenpaper_en.pdf.
5. European Commission, Directorate-General for Employment, "Green Paper: Promoting a European Framework for Corporate Social Responsibility," 8, http://europa.eu.int/comm/employment_social/soc-dial/csr/greenpaper_en.pdf.
6. Jim Collins, "The 10 Greatest CEOs of All Time: What These Extraordinary Leaders Can Teach Today's Troubled Executives," *Fortune*, July 21, 2003, 54.
7. Collins, *Good to Great*, 21.
8. Ibid., 35.
9. Joanne B. Ciulla, "Leadership Ethics: Mapping the Territory," in *Ethics: The Heart of Leadership*, ed. Joanne B. Ciulla (Westport, CT: Praeger, 1998), 12–13.
10. Joanne B. Ciulla, "Ethics and Leadership Effectiveness," in *The Nature of Leadership*, ed. John Antonakis, Anna T. Cianciolo, and Robert J. Sternberg (Thousand Oaks, CA: Sage Publications, 2004), 302–27.
11. Ibid., 310.
12. Ibid., 313.
13. Dean C. Ludwig and Clinton O. Longenecker, "The Bathsheba Syndrome: The Ethical Failure of Successful Leaders," *Journal of Business Ethics* 12 (1993): 265–73.
14. Terry L. Price, "Explaining Ethical Failures of Leadership," *Leadership and Organization Development Journal* 21 (2000): 177–84.
15. See Price's latest paper for this volume.
16. Amazon. "Book Description," *Testosterone, Inc.* http://www.amazon.com/exec/obidos/tg/detail/-/0471420050/002-3900237-4865629?v=glance&vi=reviews.
17. Kara Swisher, "Heeeere's Ronnie! He's No Longer on the Sidelines, but is Ronnie Haft Up to Leading an Empire?" *Washington Post*, November 15, 1993.
18. Kara Swisher, "Jury Awards Robert Haft $34 Million; Suit Alleged Father Wrongfully Fired Son," *Washington Post*, September 21, 1994.
19. Kara Swisher, "An Empire Builder Rebuilds His Life; Herbert Haft Says He's Happy, Despite What You've Read about His Family Troubles," *Washington Post*, October 14, 1994.
20. Stephanie Stoughton, "Stakes Rise in Hafts' Web Vitamin Duel," *Washington Post*, June 3, 1999.
21. Caroline E. Mayer and Carol D. Leonnig, "Haft Wedding Reservations; Daughter Asked Court to Block Deathbed Ceremony," *Washington Post*, September 9, 2004.
22. Albert J. Dunlap, *Mean Business: How I Save Bad Companies and Make Good Companies Great*, with Bob Andelman (New York: Times Business, 1996), xii.
23. Dunlap, *Mean Business*, 177.
24. "Jurors See Tape of Kozlowski's Party," *CNNMoney*, October 29, 2003, http://money.cnn.com/2003/10/28/news/companies/tyco_party/.
25. Kris Maher, "Scandal and Excess Make It Hard to Sell Mr. Kozlowski's Boat," *Wall Street Journal*, September 23, 2002.
26. Stanley Holmes, "Boeing: What Really Happened," *BusinessWeek*, December 15, 2003, 32.
27. Johnny Roberts and Evan Thomas, "Enron's Dirty Laundry," *Newsweek*, March 11, 2002, 22. See also Anita Raghavan, Kathryn Kranhold and Alexei Barrionuevo, "Full Speed Ahead: How Enron Bosses Created a Culture of Pushing Limits," *Wall Street Journal*, August 26, 2002.

28. Robert Bryce, *Pipe Dreams: Greed, Ego, and the Death of Enron* (New York: Public Affairs, 2002), 146.
29. Roberts and Thomas, "Enron's Dirty Laundry," *Newsweek*, March 11, 2002, 22.
30. Bryce, *Pipe Dreams*, 144.
31. Ibid., 145.
32. Ibid., 29–30.
33. Ibid., 147.
34. "Sale to Mark Lays' Exit from Aspen Real Estate," *Rocky Mountain News*, April 26, 2003.
35. Ibid.
36. Raghavan, Kranhold and Barrionuevo, "Full Speed Ahead," *Wall Street Journal*, August 26, 2002.
37. Bryce, *Pipe Dreams*,146
38. Ibid., 147–8.
39. Collins, *Good to Great*, 21–2.
40. Ibid., 5–6.
41. Ibid., 28.
42. Ibid., 35.

Index